Argentine Youth

An Untapped Potential

D1716922

THE WORLD BANK
Washington, D.C.

World Bank Country Studies are among the many reports originally prepared for internal use as part of the continuing analysis by the Bank of the economic and related conditions of its developing member countries and to facilitate its dialogs with the governments. Some of the reports are published in this series with the least possible delay for the use of governments, and the academic, business, financial, and development communities. The manuscript of this paper therefore has not been prepared in accordance with the procedures appropriate to formally-edited texts. Some sources cited in this paper may be informal documents that are not readily available.

ISBN-13: 978-0-8213-7924-0
eISBN: 978-0-8213-7925-7
ISSN: 0253-2123   DOI: 10.1596/978-0-8213-7924-0

Library of Congress Cataloging-in-Publication Data

Argentine youth : an untapped potential
    p. cm.
  Includes bibliographical references.
  ISBN 978-0-8213-7924-0
  1. Youth--Argentina--Social conditions. I. World Bank.
  HQ799.A7A744 2009
  305.2350982--dc22

                                                    2009001802

Contents

LIST OF TABLES

LIST OF FIGURES

LIST OF BOXES

Acknowledgments

The report team was managed by Dorte Verner (Task Manager). Other team members included Alessandra Heinemann, Juan Felipe Sánchez, Luis Orlando Pérez, Michael Justesen, Sergio España, Marisa Miodosky, Estanislao Gacitúa-Marió, Isabel Tomadin, Valeria Pena, Daniela Fernández, Ramón Anria, Aires Zulian Nunes da Conceicao, Susanna Shapiro, and Marisa Miodosky (all from the World Bank). Background papers were prepared by Georgina Binstock (Centro de Estudios de Población), Nicola Garcette, (Paris School of Economics), Paula Giovagnoli (Centro de Estudios Distributivos Laborales y Sociales and London School of Economics), Roxana Maurizio (Universidad Nacional de General Sarmiento), Johan Engstrom (Swedish Institute for Public Administation), Estanislao Gacitúa-Marió, Juan Felipe Sánchez, Dorte Verner, and Michael Justesen. Special thanks to the Latin American Faculty of Social Sciences and the Latin America and the Caribbean regional youth study team: Wendy Cunningham, Linda McGinnis, Cornelia Tesliuc, and Rodrigo García Verdu. The team is grateful to peer reviewers Andrea Vermehren, Linda McGinnis, and Matilde Maddaleno. It also gratefully acknowledges helpful comments and suggestions from Carter Brandon, Jesko Hentschel, McDonald Benjamin, John Nash, James Parks, José María Ghio, Gabriel Demombynes, and Elsa Anderman. The production of this report was superbly managed by Irina Ghobrial and Ramon Anria.

Vice President	Pamela Cox
Country Director	Axel van Trotsenburg/Pedro Alba
Sector Director	Laura Tuck
Sector Manager	McDonald P. Benjamin/Maninder S. Gill
Sector Leader	Carter Brandon/Franz R. Dreez-Gross
Task Manager	Dorte Verner

Acronyms and Abbreviations

AIDS	Acquired Immune Deficiency Syndrome
CCT	Conditional cash transfer
CEDES	Centro de Estudios de Estado y Sociedad
CEDLAS	Centro de Estudios Distributivos Laborales y Sociales
CEPAL	Comisión Económica para América Latina y el Caribe
DALY	Disability-adjusted life years
DINAJU	Dirección Nacional de Juventud
ECD	Early childhood development
EEJ	Educación y Empleo de los Jóvenes
EPH	Permanent Household Survey
FLACSO	Latin American Faculty of Social Sciences
GBA	Greater Buenos Aires
GDP	Gross domestic product
HIV	Human Immunodeficiency Virus
ICT	Information and communications technologies
IMF	International Monetary Fund
INDEC	Instituto Nacional de Estadística y Censos
LAC	Latin America and the Caribbean
M&E	Monitoring and evaluation
MDGs	Millennium Development Goals
NGO	Nongovernmental organization
OECD	Organisation for Economic Co-operation and Development
OLS	Ordinary least square
PISA	Programme for International Students Assessment
PROMER	Programa de Mejoramiento de la Educación Rural
SES	Socioeconomic indicator
SIPU	Swedish Institute for Public Administration
STD	Sexually-transmitted disease
UNDCP	United Nations Drug Control Program
UNESCO	United Nations Educational, Scientific and Cultural Organization
UNFPA	United Nations Population Fund
UNICEF	United Nations Children's Fund
UNODC	United Nations Office on Drugs and Crime
U.S.	United States
WDI	*World Development Indicators*
WDR	*World Development Report*
WHO	World Health Organization
YSCS	Youth Social Conditions Survey
YTP	Youth Training Program

CURRENCY EQUIVALENTS
Currency Unit = **Country Currency**
US$1 = AR$3.07
(As of June 4, 2007)

FISCAL YEAR
January 1–December 31

Executive Summary

Argentina's youth—6.7 million between the ages of 15 and 24—are an important, but to a certain extent untapped, resource for development. Over 2 million (31 percent) have already engaged in risky behaviors, and another 1 million (15 percent) are exposed to risk factors that are correlated with eventual risky behaviors. This totals 46 percent of youth at some form of risk.

Today's youth cohort is the country's largest ever and its largest for the foreseeable future. If policymakers do not invest in youth now—especially in youth at risk—they will miss a unique opportunity to equip the next generation with the abilities to become the drivers of growth, breaking the intergenerational spiral of poverty and inequality and moving Argentina back into the group of high-income countries. If youth are educated and skilled, they can be a tremendous asset for development. If not, they can burden society and public finances.

The Latin American Faculty of Social Sciences (FLACSO) and the World Bank jointly produced a new survey dataset for this report: the Youth Social Conditions Survey (YSCS; see Box 1.3 for the survey instrument). The risk behaviors and outcomes analyzed were identified through consultations with the Argentine government and youth—the report's primary audiences. The report team met on a bi-monthly basis with the majority of ministries of the Argentine federal government to consult on the work in progress. The report's objective is to generate, consolidate, and share knowledge on the risks faced by youth. The findings presented here were used as a basis for consultations with the Argentine federal government and leading universities to jointly develop policy recommendations for this final version of this report.

Although often fraught with risks, youth is also an age laden with opportunities—for youth themselves and for families, society, and the economy. Decisions about developing skills, starting on the road to financial independence, and engaging with the broader civic community will determine the quality of the next generation of workers, parents, and leaders. With more knowledge about the issues facing youth, parents, and governments can better understand and serve this group.

Overall, Argentina is blessed with high enrollment rates in school, low levels of crime and violence, and moderate to low drug use by youth. However, youth employment, smoking and binge drinking (including its effect on traffic accidents), teen pregnancies, and HIV pose challenges for youth policy. While most youth in Argentina are educated, skilled, and healthy, a large group is potentially at risk of engaging in myopic behaviors, including school absenteeism and leaving, substance use and abuse, delinquency, crime, and risky sexual behavior. The consequences of these risky behaviors—unemployment, adolescent pregnancy, sexually-transmitted diseases, addiction, incarceration, violence, and social exclusion—make it difficult for youth to successfully transition to adulthood, imposing large costs on individuals and society.

Applying the framework of the *World Development Report 2007*, this report examines the five life-changing transitions that all youth confront: leaving school and continuing to learn, starting to work, developing and maintaining a healthy lifestyle, forming a family, and exercising citizenship. Identifying risk and protective factors associated with these behaviors—individual, interpersonal, community, and societal characteristics—can inform prevention programs (World Bank 2008). Certain risky youth behaviors and negative outcomes are of particular concern:

- Early school dropout.
- Unemployment, inactivity, and informality in the workplace.
- Substance use and abuse and traffic accidents.
- Risky sexual behavior, early parenthood, and HIV/AIDS.
- Low levels of civic participation and problems of crime and violence.

Poor youth are at greatest risk—and thus a particular focus of this report. Youth make up a disproportionate share of the poor in Argentina: 31 percent of the poor are between the ages of 15 and 24, while these youth account for 17 percent of the total population. Only 24 percent of low-income students complete secondary education. Poor youth are also more likely to engage in risky sex, be victims of violence, and not participate in sports, clubs, and other organizations and cultural activities. These youth share a strong sense of injustice, believing that economic growth and state policies have not benefited them. With so many unfulfilled expectations and so little to lose, some poor youth have become disaffected (Fundación Banco de la Provincia de Buenos Aires 2005; Vommaro 2000; Garcette 2005). Many poor youth identify insecurity, inequality, and lack of political representation as critical issues (Table 1). Although youth violence in Argentina is not as prevalent or severe as in Central America or Brazil, youth—particularly poor youth—feel increasingly insecure (Kuasñosky and Szulik 1996; Rodgers 1999, 2005).

The presence of several risk factors—poverty, violence in the home, unemployment—increases the likelihood that youth will engage in risky behaviors, and risky behaviors often damage several dimensions of the transition to adulthood. School dropout is associated with early labor force entry, use or abuse of alcohol, tobacco and drugs, and increased likelihood of becoming a victim of crime. Dropouts are also more likely to engage in risky sexual behavior and to avoid participating in society, sports, and cultural activities. Risk factors are correlated, but causality may be more difficult to determine (Table 2). For example, it is not clear whether a young girl is inactive in the workforce because she has become a mother, or whether she became a mother because she was inactive.

Table 1. Top Problems Identified by Youth Ages 15–24, By Socioeconomic Strata (as a percentage of those selecting the category)

	Lack of Education	Lack of Employment	Drugs	Insecurity	Inequality	Lack of Representation
High income	16.5	9.1	10.5	9.7	9.3	11.2
Middle income	38.0	37.8	33.8	29.0	39.5	44.4
Low income	45.5	53.1	55.6	61.3	51.2	44.4
Total	100	100	100	100	100	100

Source: Calculations based on YSCS.

Table 2. Youth Behaviors and Outcomes Are Interrelated

	Inactivity (3)	Early School Dropout (3)	Early Labor Force Entry (4)	Use or Abuse of Alcohol and Tobacco (5)	Use or Abuse of Illegal Drugs (5)	Risky Sexual Behavior (6)	Victim of Crime (7)	Domestic Violence (7)	Participating in Society (7)	Involvement in Sports or Culture (7)
Inactivity (3)[a]		yes	NA	some	some	yes	yes	some	cu	little
Early school dropout (3)			yes	yes	yes	some	yes	yes	some	little
Early labor force entry (4)				some	some	yes	some	some	little	little
Use or abuse of alcohol and tobacco (5)					yes	yes	some	yes	little	some
Use or abuse of illegal drugs (5)						yes	some	yes	little	some
Risky sexual behavior (6)[b]							yes	some	little	little
Victim of crime (7)								little	some	some
Domestic violence in household (7)									some	some
Participating in society (7)[c]										yes
Involvement in sports or culture (7)										

[a]Not working or in school.
[b]Has entered parenthood.
[c]Participating in at least one organization (community, union, church, student, artistic, ecological, human rights).

Note: Numbers in parenthesis are chapters in which the area is addressed.
Source: Cluster analysis using YSCS.

Box 1: Types of Youth at Risk

More than 40 percent of youth in Argentina—2.8 million—are at risk of engaging in or suffering the consequences of risky behavior. This report categorizes youth at risk into three groups:

- ▓ Type I: Risk factors are present, but the person has not yet engaged in risky behaviors.
- ▓ Type II: Youth have engaged in risky behaviors, such as skipping school or having unprotected sex, but without serious negative consequences, such as dropping out of school, acquiring a sexual transmitted disease, or becoming pregnant.
- ▓ Type III: Youth have experienced the consequences of risky behaviors, such as teenage motherhood, dropping out of school, or incarceration.

Rewards for Investing in Youth Are Great—So Are the Costs of Inaction

With Argentina shifting toward the top-heavy demographic profile of an Organisation for Economic Co-operation and Development (OECD) country, the youth share of the population is currently peaking. Argentina's population distribution has changed from a pyramid in 1990 (many children and few old people) to a silo with more young people, adults, and elderly compared with children. The population will continue to age through falling birth rates and increasing life expectancies. Today's youth and tomorrow's youth (today's children) are the largest cohorts in Argentina.

The majority of Argentina's population will reach working age in the next five years, creating a window of opportunity to boost economic growth. These trends bring a potential demographic divided. They also bring fiscal and social challenges, some already evident. Long-term unemployment could waste human capital, while treating the results of crime, violence, drug addiction, alcoholism, and HIV/AIDS may put a heavy strain on the health care system.

Education Can Protect Youth, But Gaps in Achievement are Large

Argentines are well educated, with an advanced education system compared with most of Latin America. Argentina has made great progress since the 1980s: illiteracy has been virtually eradicated among today's youth, enrollment in primary education is nearly universal, and average educational attainment has increased, reaching 10.4 years in 2005 (compared with the regional average of 5.9 years and East Asia's average of 7.6 years). The government is to be commended for maintaining high enrollments through difficult times.

However, significant differences in educational outcomes persist by wealth and location. While less than 1 percent of 6–17-year-olds from the richest 20 percent of households are not in school, this number rises to 8.2 percent for those from the poorest 20 percent of households. Children and youth in rural areas have a higher probability of dropping out than those in urban areas.

A third of youth attending school are below the expected grade for their age. Repetition is common in Argentina, most frequently occurring in grades 1–4. Repetition—especially during early grades—can hurt outcomes. Students who repeated a year between grades 1 and 7 are less likely to attend or graduate from secondary school, and multiple repetitions compound these negative effects. Parents play an important role—youth whose parents did not complete primary education are 12 percent less likely to enroll in secondary school. Limited access to learning materials (textbooks, for example) further reduces student outcomes. High-risk groups need special attention and support to offset cumulative disadvantages.

The gains from keeping youth in school are large. Schools can be safe havens for youth, protecting them against the many harmful effects of early school dropout (Table 2): early entry into the labor market, drinking, smoking, drug use, risky sex, and becoming the victim of crime. Staying in school makes youth less likely to commit a crime, engage in risky sexual behavior, or use drugs and alcohol, and more likely to vote, play sports, and participate in clubs and cultural activities.

Economic Shocks Hit Youth Hard—And Hinder Transitions

Some Argentines start working at age 15, while others wait until their early twenties. In either case, they expect to reap the benefits of investments in education and health. An important mark of independence, the transition to the workforce is often difficult and costly. The labor market is critical for youth as a place to earn income and accumulate skills after leaving school. Unemployment deprives them of these benefits, lowering labor force participation and raising adult unemployment (World Bank 2008). Unemployment can also be a risk factor for violence and may lead to depression and other health issues.

Recent social and economic changes have heavily affected youth. For decades, entry into the labor market marked the transition to adulthood. The transition from school to the labor market, however, has become a bottleneck for many youth. They experience wider fluctuations than adults in their unemployment rate and wages, often acting as a buffer that absorbs macroeconomic shocks. Economic crisis not only reduces income levels and raises unemployment, but it often also exposes youth to other risks such as crime and violence or health hazards.

Many Argentines start working at very young ages, with severe consequences for later life. In Argentina 8.6 percent of 7–14-year-olds work exclusively, compared with 4 percent in Chile. Those who sacrifice schooling when young are more likely to be poor as adults, their productivity reduced by a lack of accumulated human capital and skills (World Bank 2006b). Early labor market entry is associated with a number of risky behaviors, including unsafe sexual activities and alcohol and tobacco use (Table 2).

Although young people are more educated today, they face difficulties entering the labor market. The informal labor market has absorbed a large share of youth that used to work in the formal sector. The unemployment rate increased between 1992 and 2003, peaking at 38.8 percent in 2002, and has since declined considerably as the economy has picked up. Youth are more than 17 percent more likely than adults to stay unemployed after having entered into unemployment. Youth unemployment is three times that of adults. Young women with low educational attainment and young informal wage earners face the highest risks.

Youth who find jobs tend to work in the informal sectors, earning less with less job security. Wage and unemployment analyses show that education contributes to higher wage returns, especially for tertiary-educated youth. Higher education also protects youth from unemployment during economic downturns. Young people, however, have far lower returns than adults to all levels of education, even controlling for experience and other factors—with youth earning on average 57 percent of the wages earned by adults. The least educated young workers face the highest job instability.

Education Is Key to Reducing Health Risks

Youth in Argentina are healthier today than ever before. But still, the probability that a 15-year-old will die before the age of 60 is higher than expected for a country of its income (90 deaths per 1,000 women and 176 deaths per 1,000 men). Probability of premature death is comparable to the levels in Uruguay and Mexico, but higher than in Chile, Italy, or Spain. This can in large part be attributed to health-related risk-taking patterns among youth.

A substantial proportion of youth in Argentina engage in risky behavior that will likely affect their well-being and productive capacity and drive up the public health burden in the future. Youth, especially young women, are starting to smoke earlier in their lives. The most likely to smoke regularly, however, are young males, youth who drink alcohol, and youth who do not attend school. Binge drinking is a problem for a significant proportion of young males (19 percent binge drink on the weekends), especially those who are not in school or who work. Excessive alcohol consumption, a risk in itself, also raises the probability of being involved in traffic accidents, smoking, engaging in risky sex, and being a victim of crime and violence.

Moreover, excessive alcohol consumption is also related to increased propensity to carry out crime and violence (including gender based violence). Illicit drug consumption is a problem primarily for youth who have dropped out of school and do not live with both parents.

Some of the risks young people take can be prevented easily and at very low cost, but health coverage among youth remains low, restricting the implementation of adequate disease prevention and control programs. Even when young people have information about the risks of certain behaviors, they continue to make choices that put their health at risk. Recently, public health interventions have focused on teaching at-risk groups life skills—how to think critically, to be assertive, and to understand the influence of community, family, and gender in decisionmaking. It is important to evaluate public health interventions carefully, focusing on changes in young people's behavior, rather than just increased knowledge, in order to learn which interventions work best in a given context.

Education stands out as a protective factor for various types of health risks, so keeping youth in school must be a priority. School attendance plays an important role delaying sexual initiation, promoting contraception use, and restraining smoking and drug use (Table 2). To be effective in reducing the future health burden, prevention programs must target youth in school as well as those who have dropped out.

Forming Families—High Stakes for Youth and the Next Generation

Reproductive health and nutrition are among the central human capital investments that facilitate a successful transition into adulthood. Adequately preparing young people for family formation and parenthood decreases fertility and dependency, facilitating human capital accumulation, productivity gains, and thus growth and poverty reduction. The intergenerational transmission of well-being is key to a more nurturing environment for the next generation. Childbearing early in life can have many negative consequences—low educational attainment, inactivity, and early entry into the labor force.

Early sexual initiation can undermine a successful transition to adulthood. Leaving school and having work experience are significant determinants of sexual initiation among men and even more so among women. The odds of sexual initiation for young women not attending school are 2.6 times those of women who are attending. Perhaps one of the gravest concerns regarding youth health arises from the low levels of consistent condom use among youth. HIV/AIDS levels are 100–200 percent higher in Argentina than among youth in Chile and Uruguay.

Some parts of Argentina, such as Chaco and Misiones, have adolescent fertility rates of more than 100 births per 1,000 people—rates comparable to Africa. Regional differences in pregnancy rates suggest that context, such as values toward gender and maternity, has an important effect on young people's reproductive decisions. Youth from less privileged socioeconomic backgrounds are the most exposed to unplanned pregnancies, and young women whose mothers have not completed high school are twice as likely to become pregnant. In Latin America 52 percent of pregnancies are unplanned and 23 percent end in abortion. Illegal in Argentina, abortions are often performed under unsanitary and unsafe conditions, resulting in infection, hemorrhage, and sometimes death.

Because later sexual initiation, delayed marriage, lower pregnancy rates, and greater use of contraceptives are closely linked to higher educational attainment, school attendance in poor and rural areas should be encouraged, especially among women. Furthermore, sex education programs can teach youth the necessary life skills to make sound decisions and negotiate safe sexual behavior with peers and partners.

Youth Can Change Society for the Better

Youth participation and civic engagement encourages long-term political stability, good governance, and better accountability, but disengaged youth can pose a number of risks for society, including increased violence, crime, drug addiction, and social instability. This is particularly true in times of social crises, when opportunities decrease sharply for less advantaged groups and social differences are most marked. Alternative channels of mobilization and political participation have emerged. The *piqueteros* and *barras bravas* movements—appealing particularly to marginalized youth—have organized youth around their social exclusion.

Unemployment—most harmful to low-income youth—has hindered the transition to adulthood for many, leading to social exclusion and impeding the development of full citizenship for those affected. Poor youth have also suffered from limited access to health care and services provided by the state. Lacking integration through the educational system, labor markets, or state services, some youth have become isolated and alienated. Because appropriate channels for participation within the politico-institutional arena are sometimes limited, low-income youth are poorly represented in civil and political institutions and policymaking and tend to have lower voter participation rates.

Although Argentina has worked to advance human rights for children and youth internationally and has had some success experimenting with alternative models of juvenile justice, youth incarceration rates are high, indicating that these approaches have not yet permeated the juvenile justice system. Becoming the victim of crime—or its perpetrator—severely inhibits the ability of youth to transition to responsible adult citizenship. Violence is also extremely costly to society—in medical bills, lower productivity, and policing and incarceration costs. Most criminal careers begin in adolescence, making a compelling case for focusing crime prevention efforts on youth and offering feasible rehabilitation options to those who have committed offenses. Unfortunately, young offenders—often dismissed as lost causes—tend to be treated the same way as adults.

Easing the transition of poor and marginal youth to full citizenship can be achieved through economic, social, and political empowerment. The potentially positive impact of youth on economic and social change may be squandered if they are isolated economically, socially, and psychologically. Facilitating youth engagement in community development activities and transferring resources and decisionmaking responsibilities to youth is likely to contribute to better governance and accountability. Bringing youth into community activities forges a common vision and sense of identity, increasing solidarity and trust. Building the capacity of state institutions at different levels to address youth issues and facilitate youth participation in policymaking is a critical challenge.

Policy Directions to Reduce Youth at Risk

Because youth respond to their environment, it is sensible to focus on getting the environment right by combating risk factors and promoting protective factors. A number of evaluated programs show that these goals can be achieved even under tight fiscal constraints, for instance by expanding early childhood development and gearing the school environment toward lifelong learning and citizenship. Targeting poor youth is essential for maximum effectiveness (McGinnis 2007).

A mixed portfolio of programs and interventions, some specific to youth and some more broadly focused, is required to achieve a balance between short-run targeting of those already suffering negative consequences of risky behaviors—such as second chance programs and rehabilitation for youth already "stuck"—and long-run prevention for other youth to keep them from engaging in risky behaviors (McGinnis 2007).

By focusing policies and programs on the individual (improving life skills, self-esteem), on key relationships (parents, caregivers, peers), on communities (schools, neighborhoods, police), and on societal laws and norms, the chance of reducing the numbers of youth at risk over the long term is greatest.

Specific recommendations were developed during consultations with government counterparts. As a basis for discussions, a basic strategy should consider the following.

1. Investing earlier in life and expanding youth opportunities

- Prevention strategies and programs are effective not only in developing the potential of young people, but also in addressing both early and late onset of risky behaviors. Improving and expanding existing interventions will broaden opportunities for young people to develop their human capital.
- Consideration could be given to: i) Scaling up existing early child development to reach most children 0–3 years of age; ii) Improving education so that young people are able to complete secondary school and have better basic skills for further learning, job placement, and practical living; iii) Enhancing the information available

to young people to make the right decisions regarding their health and life choices (reproductive health, HIV/AIDS; substance abuse; conflict resolution/violence prevention; participation).

2. Targeting at-risk youth more effectively

- Moving away from zero tolerance (or *mano dura*) and toward comprehensive youth development has proven successful and cost-effective.
- Addressing risk and protective factors, with a focus on providing second chances (or in some cases rehabilitation) to youth already at some form of risk, has been an effective approach.
- Areas that might be given consideration could include: i) Scaling up cash transfer programs for disadvantaged youth (for example, cash transfers conditional on completing secondary school and reducing specific risky behaviors); ii) Establishing degree equivalence systems, recognized by the formal education system; iii) Investing in youth service programs—actively engaging young people in the delivery of social services and public works, especially at the neighborhood and community level; iv) Supporting after-school activities and mentoring services; v) Scaling up internship, training, and employment information services targeted to at-risk youth.

3. Influencing policies that are not youth-specific

- In addition to the policies directly targeted at youth, many policies have an important impact on them, even if youth are not the primary target. These policies focus on the community and on some of the broader contexts affecting youth.
- Among interventions that might be considered are: i) Promoting labor market reforms that balance job protection with the flexibility to encourage job creation and that improve the conditions in the informal sector; ii) Focusing micro-credit/micro-enterprise programs to create economic opportunities and generate employment for youth; iii) Strengthening the police and justice system responses to reflect age-specific needs and priorities of the young and enhance their rights; iv) Building safer neighborhoods and communities, combining improved urban designs, social services, community policing, and traffic and road safety; v) Limiting the availability of alcohol and tobacco and reducing the availability of firearms.

To achieve success, these strategies require strong cross-sector, multi-stakeholder collaboration among ministries, the justice system, municipalities, police, military, courts, prisons, media, community-based organizations, youth organizations, parents, rights-based nongovernmental organizations, schools, universities, sports clubs, private enterprises, and churches.

4. Making public policy work for youth

Positively influencing youth transitions and having a successful mix of policies and interventions directed at youth requires decisive action that ensures coherence of youth goals and policies with development goals and policies. For example:

- Improving data for more effective targeting and implementation—including dis-aggregated age-specific data on households and specialized surveys (for example, victimization surveys in low-income areas).

- Ensuring that young people have a voice in designing and implementing policies and interventions that affect them (thereby encouraging effective youth participation and engagement)—including recognizing youth as key stakeholders for development, expanding their options for engagement at the national and local levels, and supporting youth service and youth-led initiatives.

- Enhancing coordination and having clear lines of accountability across policies and sectors that affect youth—including strengthening youth focal points tasked with the responsibility of identifying youth development synergies, opportunities for cross-sector collaborations and coordination, facilitation of action plans and budgets, and monitoring and evaluation.

- Improving monitoring and evaluation—compiling basic youth indicators; monitoring progress in the implementation of cross-sector interventions; carrying out effective evaluations that emphasize the identification of both the spillover effects from one youth transition to another and the complementarities across transitions.

5. Engaging youth for better accountability and governance

Youth inclusion and participation in public policy gives young people more choices, enhances their capabilities, and improves their lives, as well as those of their communities. Integrating youth into the development process as stakeholders and decisionmakers—from consultations to policy, from implementation to evaluation—gives them ownership of the policies and interventions that affect them and enhances national and local development processes.

Interventions should also involve youth in delivering assets to others. Youth service programs can: (i) Empower youth to play an active role in the development of their community and the country; (ii) Help them acquire the experience, knowledge, skills, and values necessary for employment and active citizenship; (iii) Provide constructive alternatives to risky behaviors an d reintegrate marginalized youth; and (iv) Be an important and cost-effective tool in addressing a wide range of development priorities (for example, combating HIV/AIDS).

CHAPTER 1

Introduction

By Dorte Verner

> "I represent a group of young people from the outlying suburbs who work because they have to help their families. In many cases these are families where the parents are separated and the young people are taking care of their families. It's like switching roles. Young people don't do work that they like, they work because they have to in order to survive."
>
> —Susana, 23 years old, Posadas.

It is critical for policymakers in Argentina to address youth issues, even when they face so many other demands. With 17 percent (6.7 million) of Argentina's population between the ages of 15 and 24, the current youth cohort is the largest Argentina has ever had—and its largest for the foreseeable future. Youth are a huge, but to a certain extent untapped, resource for development. If youth are educated and skilled, they can be a tremendous asset. If not, they can burden society and public finances. The majority of youth in Argentina make good decisions and are educated, skilled, and healthy. Youth have low crime and violence rates, moderate to low drug abuse, and an active—but moderate—movement (*piqueteros*) through which they are engaging politically.

But 46 percent of Argentina's youth are at risk. Over 2 million (31 percent) have already engaged in risky behaviors, and another 1 million (15 percent) are exposed to key risk factors that are correlated with eventual risky behaviors (see Chapter 2). At-risk youth face environmental, social, and family conditions that hinder their personal development and their successful integration into society as productive citizens. They have—relative to their peers—an increased propensity to engage in risky behavior, including school absenteeism and leaving, substance use and abuse, delinquency, crime, and risky sexual behavior (see Chapter 2 and Box 1.1 for definitions; World Bank 2008). The consequences of these risky behaviors—unemployment, adolescent pregnancy, sexually-transmitted diseases, addiction, incarceration, violence, and social exclusion—make it

---

Box 1.1: Definitions and Concepts

Youth

This report defines youth as ages 15–24, but this category is merely a proxy for the stage in a young person's life when he or she transitions from dependence (childhood) to independence (adulthood).

Youth at risk

At-risk youth face environmental, social, and family conditions that hinder their personal development and their successful integration into society as productive citizens. They have—relative to their peers—an increased propensity to engage in risky behaviors. The consequences of these risky behaviors make it difficult for these youth to successfully transition to adulthood.

Risk and protective factors

Risk factors increase the likelihood that a young person will experience negative outcomes (for example, youth who experience physical or sexual abuse in their homes are more likely to engage in violence and other risky behaviors themselves). Protective factors reduce the chances of negative outcomes and increase the likelihood that a young person will transition successfully to adulthood (for example, youth school attendance and social connectedness are among the most important protective factors in reducing the risks of many behaviors; Blum and others 2003; World Bank 2003; Blum and Ireland 2004; Ohene, Ireland, and Blum 2005; Udry 2003). Although not necessarily causal, these risk and protective factors can be important predictors (McGinnis 2007).

Risk situations

Youth fall into three types of risk situations discussed in this report.

- Type I: Risk factors are present, but the person has not yet engaged in risky behaviors.
- Type II: Youth have engaged in risky behaviors, such as skipping school or having unprotected sex, but without serious negative consequences.
- Type III: Youth have experienced the consequences of risky behaviors, such as teenage motherhood, dropping out of school, or incarceration.

---

difficult for youth to transition successfully to adulthood. These potentially devastating outcomes, which are costly to individuals and to society, motivate this report's focus on youth at risk.

If policymakers do not invest in youth now—especially in youth at risk—they will miss a unique opportunity to equip the next generation with the abilities to become the drivers of growth, breaking the intergenerational spiral of poverty and inequality and moving Argentina back into the group of high-income countries (Verner and Alda 2004). East Asia provides an instructive example: more than 40 percent of the high growth in East Asia in 1965–90 was due to the fast growth of its working-age population and strong polices for trade and human capital development (Bloom and Canning 2005).

Those at greatest risk—and thus a particular focus of this report—are poor youth. A significant number of these youth share a strong sense of injustice, believing that economic growth and state policies have not benefited them. With so many unfulfilled expectations and so little to lose, some poor youth have become disaffected (Fundación Banco de la Provincia de Buenos Aires 2005; Vommaro 2000; Garcette 2005). A large proportion of poor youth identify insecurity, inequality, and lack of political representation as the critical

Table 1.1. Top Problems Identified By Youth Ages 15–24, By Socioeconomic Strata (as a percentage of those selecting the category)

	Lack of Education	Lack of Employment	Drugs	Insecurity	Inequality	Lack of Representation
High income	16.5	9.1	10.5	9.7	9.3	11.2
Middle income	38.0	37.8	33.8	29.0	39.5	44.4
Low income	45.5	53.1	55.6	61.3	51.2	44.4
Total	100	100	100	100	100	100

Source: Calculations based on YSCS.

issues they face (Table 1.1). Although youth violence in Argentina is not as prevalent or severe as in Central America or Brazil, poor youth increasingly feel insecure (Kuasñosky and Szulik 1996; Rodgers 1999, 2005).

The Latin American Faculty of Social Sciences (FLACSO) and the World Bank jointly produced a new survey dataset for this report: the Youth Social Conditions Survey (YSCS). The World Bank developed the survey instrument and FLACSO carried out the data collection (see Box 1.3). A series of innovative analyses provided the basis for background papers produced on education, health, labor markets, federal programs, citizenship, and crime and violence. This report uses the analysis and framework developed for the *World Development Report 2007* and the Regional Youth Study for Latin America and the Caribbean (see Box 1.2; World Bank 2006b, 2008).

The report is based on consultations with the majority of the ministries in the Argentine federal government (MESA). The team and MESA held bimonthly meetings to consult on the work. These meetings first addressed the study's concept and the issues it would tackle. They then focused on presenting and discussing the health, education, and crime and violence background papers. Labor market background papers were presented and discussed in subsequent meetings. Furthermore, a meetings to consult on the draft report and jointly develop policy recommendations took place.

The risk behaviors and outcomes analyzed in this report have been identified through consultations with the Argentine government and youth—the report's primary audiences. The report's objective is to generate, consolidate, and share knowledge and information on the risks faced by youth and the policy options for addressing them. This report defines youth as ages 15–24,[1] but this category is merely a proxy for the stage in a young person's life when he or she transitions from dependence (childhood) to independence (adulthood).[2] This stage involves the challenges of transitioning from school to work, moving from being single to forming a family, avoiding risks to health, and engaging as a citizen.

---

1. This definition is consistent with that of the United Nations Millennium Development Goals.

2. The *World Development Report 2007* uses the 12–24 age category because, in many low-income countries, a large share of youth start the transition to adulthood earlier than in middle- or high-income countries.

Blum and others (2003); World Bank (2003); Blum and Ireland (2004); Ohene, Ireland, and Blum (2005); Udry (2003).

Certain risky youth behaviors and negative outcomes are of particular concern in Argentina:

- Early school dropout.
- Unemployment, inactivity, or informality in the workplace.
- Substance use/abuse and traffic accidents.
- Risky sexual behavior, early parenthood, and HIV/AIDS.
- Civic participation, crime, and violence.

Identifying risk and protective factors associated with these behaviors can indicate contributing factors—individual, interpersonal, community, and societal characteristics—which can then inform prevention programs (World Bank 2008). Risk factors such as poverty increase the likelihood that a young person will experience negative outcomes. Furthermore, youth who experience physical or sexual abuse in their homes are more likely to engage in violence and other risky behaviors themselves. If they also drop out of school, the chances of negative outcomes increase significantly.

Protective factors reduce the chances of negative outcomes and increase the likelihood that a young person will transition successfully to adulthood. For example, school attendance and social connectedness are among the most important protective factors in reducing substance abuse (alcohol, cigarettes, marijuana), violent or deviant behavior, early sexual initiation, and pregnancy among secondary school students (Blum and others 2003; World Bank 2003; Blum and Ireland 2004; Ohene, Ireland, and Blum 2005; Udry 2003).

Although not necessarily causal, these risk and protective factors can be important predictors. With different effects at different stages of development, they often appear in clusters, multiplying the positive or negative effects (Table 1.2). The more risk factors confronting youth, the more likely it becomes that they will engage in risk behaviors. And the more protective factors in the lives of youth, the more likely it is that they will make successful transitions to adulthood (McGinnis 2007).

At-risk youth need special attention because risky behaviors are costly to youth and to society. Although this report focuses on the external aspects of youth transitions (to parenthood, to employment, to citizenship), youth is also a period of internal, psychological transitions—a period of breaking free from parents through independent thinking, of searching for recognition and respect among peers, of sexual awakening, of increased competition with others over resources, of emphasis on the present over the future, and of relatively few responsibilities to others. Youth, however, have little experience addressing these issues. They often behave in ways that are rational for their objectives and perceptions of risk—especially given frustrations with economic turbulence, blocked participation, and marginalization in the community—but that are considered risky from society's viewpoint and that incur significant costs to themselves, to society, and to the economy. For example, a 14-year-old girl who dropped out of school and has limited employment prospects said: "Now I am a mother; the community respects me and sees me as a mother. Do I know about contraceptives? Yes, of course, but using them does not get me a job or respect among people in the community. My daughter does give me respect because I am now a mother."

Table 1.2. Youth Behaviors and Outcomes Are Interrelated

	Inactivity (3)[a]	Early school dropout (3)	Early labor force entry (4)	Use or abuse of alcohol and tobacco (5)	Use or abuse of illegal drugs (5)[b]	Risky sexual behavior (6)[b]	Victim of crime (7)	Domestic violence in household (7)	Participating in society (7)[c]	Involvement in sports or culture (7)
Involvement in Sports or Culture (7)	little	little	little	some	some	little	some	some	yes	
Participating in Society (7)	no	some	little	little	little	little	some	some		
Domestic Violence (7)	some	yes	some	yes	yes	some	little			
Victim of Crime (7)	yes	yes	yes	some	some	yes				
Risky Sexual Behavior (6)	yes	some	yes	yes	yes					
Use or Abuse of Illegal Drugs (5)	some	yes	some	yes						
Use or Abuse of Alcohol and Tobacco (5)	some	yes	some							
Early Labor Force Entry (4)	NA	yes								
Early School Dropout (3)	yes									
Inactivity (3)										

[a] Not working or in school.

[b] Has entered parenthood.

[c] Participating in at least one organization (community, union, church, student, artistic, ecological, human rights).

Note: Numbers in parenthesis are chapters in which the area is addressed.

Source: Cluster analysis using YSCS.

Box 1.2: World Development Report 2007 and the Regional Youth Study for Latin America and the Caribbean

---

The theme of the *World Development Report 2007* (WDR) is youth, ages 12 to 24. It focuses on decisions concerning the five phases with the biggest long-term impact on how human capital is kept safe, developed, and deployed. For each phase (continuing to learn, starting to work, developing a healthful lifestyle, beginning a family, and exercising citizenship) governments must increase investments directly and cultivate an environment for young people and their families to invest in themselves. The WDR suggests that a youth lens on policies affecting the five phases would help focus on three broad directions: expanding opportunities, enhancing capabilities, and providing second chances. Each pathway (opportunities, capabilities, and second chances) is applied to each of the transitions, generating reform suggestions. To mobilize the economic and political resources to stimulate such reforms, countries must resolve three issues: better coordination and integration with national policy, stronger voice, and more evaluation. In addition, the WDR examines both youth migration, and their increasing use of new technologies.

The recently released 2007 Regional Youth study, entitled *The Promise of Youth: Policy for Youth at Risk in Latin America and the Caribbean,* narrows the scope of research to focus on "at risk" youth in Latin America and the Caribbean, a group that makes up over 50 percent of the region's population ages 15–24. This report offers the following four key recommendations to improve opportunities and well-being of this group: (1) Immediately scale up "targeted prevention" programs and efforts, with particular emphasis on expanding integrated early childhood development for children from poor households; increasing attention to secondary school completion; using schools and media as vehicles for important messages and information; and promoting effective parenting; (2) Move ahead cautiously on "second chance" and "rehabilitation" programs including educational equivalency, job training, conditional cash transfers, youth service, mentoring, and others; (3) Pay attention to policies that may not focus on youth but have disproportionate effects on at-risk youth, such as cigarette taxes, the justice system (which could focus on treating rather than incarcerating youth), alcohol sales, and providing birth registration for the undocumented; (4) Reallocate resources away from youth programs proven to be ineffective. The report concludes by mentioning several cross-cutting themes, such as the need for better monitoring and evaluation systems, and the fact that youth themselves must be involved and empowered to take ownership of their futures and that of their communities.

The individual and societal costs of risky behavior are high. A young woman who leaves school early earns on average $28,273 less over her lifetime than if she had finished secondary school—a young man earns $30,475 less.[3] The cost to Argentine society is an additional $5.3 billion. The effect on GDP is considerable: it is 2.7 percent lower because of individuals leaving secondary school early.

Although fraught with risks, youth is also an age laden with opportunities—for youth themselves and for families, society, and the economy. Decisions about developing skills, starting on the road to financial independence, and engaging with the broader civic community will determine the quality of the next generation of workers, parents, and leaders (World Bank 2006b) With more knowledge about the issues facing youth, parents and governments may be better able to understand and serve this group.

The report is organized in eight chapters. Chapter 2 provides the framework and definitions used throughout the report, along with demographic data. Chapters 3–7 focus on

---

3. World Bank (2008). Calculations are based on a working life of 45 years, with a discount rate of 5 percent (see Assuncão 2005).

Box 1.3: Data Used for Analyses

The key data sets in this report are the Youth Social Conditions Survey (YSCS), the National House-hold Survey (EPH—Permanent Household Survey), the youth education and employment survey (EEJ—Educación y Empleo de los Jóvenes; a special 2005 supplement to the EPH), and the *World Development Indicators* (WDI).

The YSCS was developed for this report by the World Bank and carried out by the Latin American Faculty of Social Sciences (FLACSO) in December 2005. This survey was conducted in four metro-politan areas—Buenos Aires, Misiones, Salta, and Neuquén—and interviewed youth ages 15–24 in their homes. The advantage of home interviews is that they include youth who have dropped out of school, while school interviews do not. The sample was developed following the sampling frame of the EPH.[4]

The YSCS provides information on a broad range of issues: demographics, education, leisure, autonomy, community participation, security and conflict, labor participation, health and use of drugs, characteristics of the dwelling, and perceptions about youth-related problems. The survey interviewed 1,289 males and females.[5] Supplementary information on parents or guardians living in the same household was collected for 710 adults.[6]

The EEJ survey—produced by the Center for the Study of Distribution, Labor, and Social Affairs (CEDLAS) and carried out by Instituto Nacional de Estadística y Censos in 2005—includes a wide range of questions that enable following student progress in education. A module specific to young people (15–30-years old) living in greater Buenos Aires, the EEJ was introduced into the EPH to cap-ture educational paths, family backgrounds, and labor market experiences. The survey lacked national coverage, but greater Buenos Aires accounts for 30 percent of students in the country.

---

the five youth transitions: Chapter 3 addresses education, school dropout, and continued learning; Chapter 4 deals with labor markets and business cycles; Chapter 5 addresses health, including substance use/abuse; Chapter 6 discusses family formation, including risky sexual behavior, early pregnancy, and HIV/AIDS; and Chapter 7 deals with citizenship, participation, and crime and violence. Chapter 8 offers youth policy suggestions as tenta-tive areas for further consultation and discussion.

---

4. For more detailed information about the characteristics of the sample and the fieldwork, see FLACSO (2006).

5. The number of youth interviewed in greater Buenos Aires was 347, in Posadas 313, in Neuquén 282, and in Salta 347.

6. Data could come from the father, the mother, or another adult in the household.

CHAPTER 2

Demographics and Framework

By Dorte Verner

"It seems to me that social violence has increased. It's a feeling of impotence. They treat you bad, or vice versa, you treat others bad. I think it's got something to do with that."

—Martin, 22 years old, political science student, city of Buenos Aires.

With the majority of Argentina's population reaching working age in the next five years, a window of opportunity is opening to boost economic growth. But this will happen only if youth are educated and able to obtain good jobs, making investments in human capital imperative. The demographic dividend of falling dependency and rising labor force participation can be large, but the costs can be equally great if youth fail to find jobs. To minimize the risks to youth, it is sensible to invest in them now. Because today's young people will become the next generation of parents and workers, intergenerational effects will compound the dividends of today's investments—or the costs of inaction from rising risks to youth.

To lay the foundation for the rest of the report, this chapter reviews the demographic situation in Argentina. Not intended to be comprehensive, it instead outlines the main demographic factors affecting youth. The chapter then presents a framework for analyzing at-risk youth.

Demographics

In Argentina 6.7 million people are between the ages of 15 and 24 (17 percent of the population). While the youth share of the population is high compared with the Organisation for Economic Co-operation and Development (OECD) countries, it is one of the lowest in Latin America and the Caribbean. Youth constitute only 12 percent of the population in

Table 2.1. Youth Ages 15–24 in 2005, Selected Countries

Country	Population (millions)	Youth Share of Population (%)	Share of the Youth Population in LAC (%)
Argentina			
Both sexes	39.5	17.0	6.5
Male	19.5	17.4	6.5
Female	20.0	16.6	6.5
Bolivia	8.9	21.4	1.8
Brazil	186.1	18.8	33.7
Chile	16.0	17.0	2.6
Colombia	43.0	17.7	7.3
Ecuador	13.4	19.8	2.5
Mexico	106.2	19.0	19.5
Paraguay	6.3	18.6	1.1
Peru	27.9	18.6	5.0
Uruguay	3.4	15.2	0.5
Venezuela	25.4	19.1	4.7
Latin America and the Caribbean	555.0	18.7	
Denmark	5.4	11.1	
Spain	40.3	11.6	
Sweden	9.0	12.6	
United States	295.7	14.2	

Source: Calculations based on World Bank (2005c).

Spain, 14 percent in the United States, and 16.9 percent in Chile (Table 2.1). Young women in Argentina make up a smaller share of the female population than young men do of the male population, mainly because of women's longer life expectancies (78 years for women compared with 71 years for men in 2003; World Bank 2005c).

Like most other countries, Argentina's fertility rate has fallen and life expectancy has increased (Figure 2.1). Women now complete more schooling and enter the labor market in greater numbers, which has encouraged family planning and reduced fertility. Better health services and nutrition have increased life expectancies.[7] These changes have diminished the share of children (ages 0–14) compared with that of other groups.

With Argentina shifting toward the top-heavy demographic profile of an OECD country, the youth share of the population is currently peaking. Argentina's population distribution has changed from a pyramid in 1990 (many children and few old people) to a silo with more young people, adults, and elderly compared with children (Figures 2.2 and 2.3).[8]

---

7. Net migration, however, has been negative since 2000 (World Bank 2006a).

8. Jimeno and Rodríguez-Palenzuela (2002) find that a rapid increase in youth population size and ensuing declines in fertility rates are positively associated with fluctuations in relative youth unemployment rates. Chapter 4 shows this has been the case in Argentina.

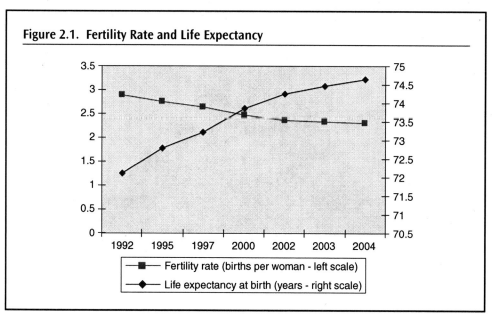

Figure 2.1. Fertility Rate and Life Expectancy

Source: Calculations based on *World Development Indicators*, various years.

The population will continue to age through falling birth rates and increasing life expectancies. Today's youth and tomorrow's coming youth (children) are the largest cohorts in Argentina. But the number of young people in Argentina is now at its height—the child cohort (ages 0–15) is becoming smaller than the youth cohort because of falling fertility rates, and projections show that it will continue to shrink. The fertility decline will produce a "bulge" in the population around 2020 (Figures 2.4 and 2.5).

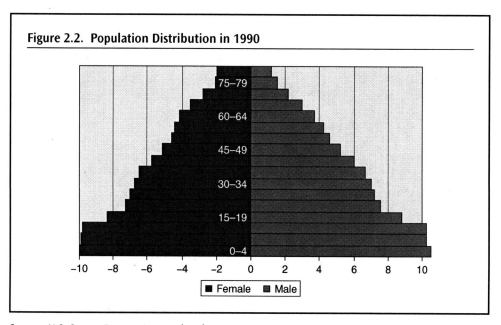

Figure 2.2. Population Distribution in 1990

Source: U.S. Census Bureau, International Data Base.

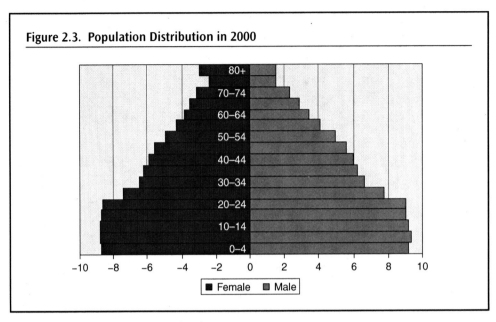

Figure 2.3. Population Distribution in 2000

Source: U.S. Census Bureau, International Data Base.

The majority of Argentine youth live in the greater capital region, Pampeana. The Pampeana and greater Buenos Aires region is home to 65 percent of youth in Argentina, with only 5 percent in Patagonia and 7 percent in Cuyo (Figure 2.6). Pampeana and greater Buenos Aires, however, are also the areas with the lowest proportions of youth in the population (17 percent). In the Northwest and Northeast regions, 19 percent of the population is 15 to 24 years old. Pampeana is leading the demographic transition, while the less populated

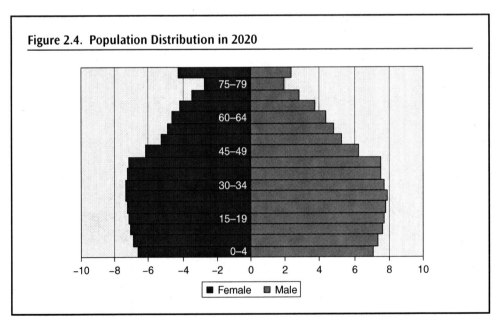

Figure 2.4. Population Distribution in 2020

Source: U.S. Census Bureau, International Data Base.

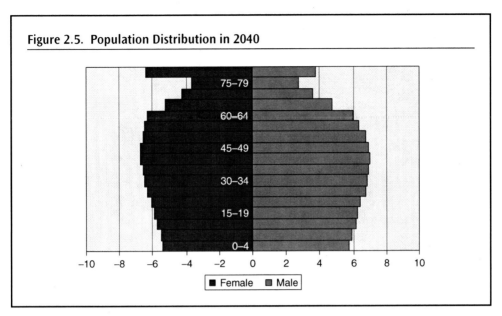

Figure 2.5. Population Distribution in 2040

Source: U.S. Census Bureau, International Data Base.

and developed regions lag behind. So even though there are fewer youth in the north and Patagonia, they are a larger constituency in these regions (Figure 2.7).

The older cohorts, particularly older women, have become a larger part of the population. This trend is expected to continue. By 2040 the cohort of women older than 80 will outnumber the youngest cohorts. An aging population will create a demographic burden, with relatively few workers to support children and the elderly, requiring adjustments in the labor market and social services. Argentina should take advantage of the current opportunity to boost economic growth. The large proportion of youth can increase productivity and reduce the demographic burden—provided youth have access to education and jobs (World Bank 2006b).

If Argentina can absorb the growing cohorts of new workers, it can boost growth and earn a demographic dividend. The growth in per capita labor supply, reinforced by rising female labor force participation, increases output per capita. And a larger working-age population is correlated with higher per capita savings and investment (World Bank 2008). Indeed, more than 40 percent of East Asia's edge over Latin America in growth in 1965–90 stemmed from faster growth in its working-age population and better polices for trade and human capital development (Bloom and Canning 2005). Therefore, it is prudent to focus on economic fundamentals in order to generate the jobs necessary to employ the largest youth cohort ever. Not doing so can increase the number of youth at risk, incurring large costs for society and the economy.

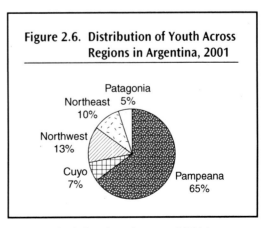

Figure 2.6. Distribution of Youth Across Regions in Argentina, 2001

Source: Calculations based on INDEC (2001).

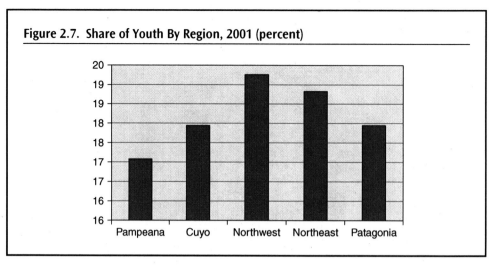

Figure 2.7. Share of Youth By Region, 2001 (percent)

Source: Calculations based on INDEC (2001).

The demographic changes will also bring fiscal and social challenges, some already evident. The per-pupil cost of secondary education, already higher than that of primary education, has risen. Long-term unemployment could waste human capital. Treating the results of crime, violence, drug addiction, alcoholism, and HIV/AIDS (with young people, particularly young men, accounting for nearly half of all new infections) may strain the health care system.

The Framework

The need for Argentina to invest in its youth is clear. Making sound investments requires understanding the risks facing youth. This section presents a framework to inform the analysis and policy directions that follow. Applying the framework of the *World Development Report 2007*, this report examines the five life-changing transitions that all youth confront: leaving school and continuing to learn, starting to work, developing and maintaining a healthy lifestyle, forming a family, and exercising citizenship (Figure 2.8).

Children start responding to influences at birth. They learn behaviors, both positive and negative, from parents and peers, in school, and in the community. Risks increase dramatically as they reach ages 15–24. Youth are engaging in risky behaviors earlier than previous generations and the behaviors are often more dangerous: unprotected sex did not potentially lead to HIV/AIDS infection 30 years ago. Moreover, these behaviors tend to cluster—youth engaged in one are likely to engage in others (Box 2.1). These clustered behaviors are then passed on to the next generation. However, if youth are protected and do not engage in risky behaviors, the positive effects on the next generation are maximized.

Poor youth are most at risk, and 31 percent of the poor in Argentina are between 15 and 24 (World Bank 2001). For instance, only 24 percent of low-income students complete secondary education. Poor youth are also more likely to engaging in risky sexual behaviors, be victims of violence, and not participate in sports, clubs, and other organizations or cultural activities.

This report categorizes at-risk youth into three types:

■ Type I: Risk factors are present, but the person has not yet engaged in risky behaviors.

Figure 2.8. Five Youth Transitions to Adulthood

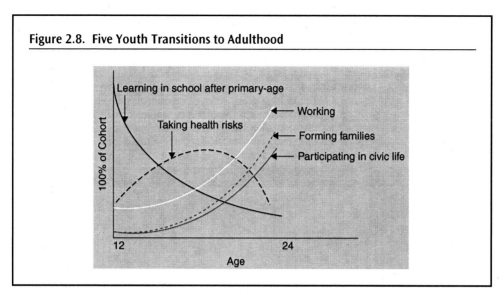

Source: World Bank (2006b).

- ▓ Type II: Youth have engaged in risky behaviors, such as skipping school or having unprotected sex, but without serious negative consequences, such as dropping out of school, acquiring a sexually-transmitted disease, or becoming pregnant.
- ▓ Type III: Youth have experienced the consequences of risky behaviors, such as teenage motherhood, dropping out of school, or incarceration.

Although the majority of youth in Argentina are not at risk (53.6 percent), most of the at-risk population is at Type III risk (24.9 percent), meaning that they are experiencing the consequences of risky behaviors (Table 2.2).[9] Fifteen percent of youth have not yet engaged in risky behaviors, but risk factors are present in their lives (Type I). They tend to live in a less secure neighborhoods (some have been victims of violence) and tend to come from lower income households than those who are not at risk. Yet, some play sports and are members of a cultural organization or club, and the vast majority attend school—all protective factors. Six percent of youth are engaging in risky behaviors—starting to smoke, drink, have unprotected sex, and skip classes—without major negative consequences, such as dropping out of school and becoming pregnant (Type II). A quarter of Argentine youth are experiencing the consequences of risky behaviors (Type III): dropping out of school, entering parenthood, and becoming HIV positive (see Table 1.2).[10] As effects are cumulative, these youth often face more than one risk.

No single factor can explain why some youth are more likely to undertake risky behaviors than their peers. Identifying which factors have the greatest impact on youth behavior

---

9. See the LAC Regional Youth Study (World Bank 2008). Cluster analyses are intended largely for generating information rather than testing hypotheses.

10. The analysis of the Regional Youth Study (World Bank 2008) study concludes that poverty is a good proxy to measure at-risk youth. This can be measured or proxied by the level of parents' education, household durables and assets, and household income.

Box 2.1: Conceptual Framework for Youth at Risk

Risk factors—abuse in the home, limited employment opportunities, poverty, and so on—contribute to risky behaviors, such as skipping school, early sexual initiation, and substance abuse. Risk factors and risky behaviors—often occurring in clusters—can lead to negative outcomes (incarceration, acquiring sexually-transmitted diseases, school dropout). Such obstacles hinder young people from making successful transitions to adulthood by finding jobs, becoming responsible parents, caring for their health, and participating in the community and politics. Understanding these linkages enables policymakers to consider concrete policy and programmatic options for reducing the population of youth at risk.

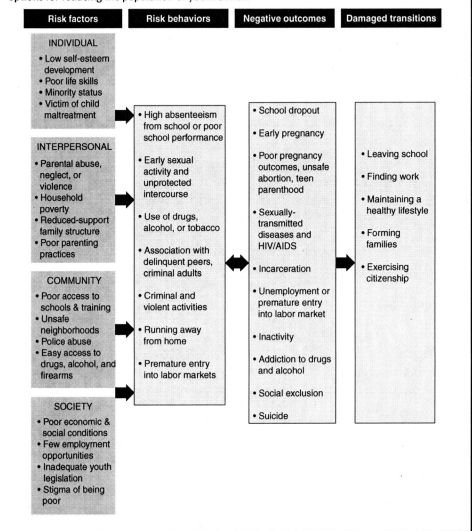

Source: World Bank (2006b) and McGinnis (2007).

and outcomes—and their subsequent adult outcomes—can provide policymakers with a useful framework to guide policy and programmatic choices.

Because the presence of several risk factors increases the likelihood that youth will engage in risky behavior, one can look at the association between different factors—though

Table 2.2. Youth in Argentina, By Risk Status (percent)

	Not At Risk	At Risk Type I	At Risk Type II	At Risk Type III
Argentina	53.6	15.1	6.4	24.9

Source: Calculations based on YSCS, see appendix II.

causality may be more difficult to determine (see Table 1.2). For example, it is not clear whether a young girl is inactive in the workforce because she has become a mother, or whether she became a mother because she was inactive.

So what can be done to reduce the likelihood that youth will engage in risky behaviors? Because youth respond to their environment, it is sensible to focus on combating risk factors and promoting protective factors. A number of evaluated programs show that something can be done even under tight fiscal constraints, such as expanding early childhood development and gearing the school environment toward lifelong learning and citizenship. Moreover, evidence shows that targeting poor youth is essential and that it is prudent to move away from zero tolerance (or *mano dura*) and toward a comprehensive youth development model (McGinnis 2007).

A mixed portfolio of programs and interventions is necessary to achieve a balance between short-run targeting of those already suffering negative consequences of risky behaviors (Type III)—such as second chance programs and rehabilitation for youth already "stuck"—and long-run prevention for other youth (Types I and II) to keep them from engaging in risky behaviors (McGinnis 2007). By focusing policies and programs on the individual (improving life skills, self-esteem), on key relationships (parents, caregivers, peers), on communities (schools, neighborhoods, police), and on societal laws and norms, the chance of reducing the numbers of youth at risk over the long term is greatest.

CHAPTER 3

Education and Learning

By Paula Giovagnoli and Dorte Verner

"What often happens is that you have a job you know will last three months, and you think 'Well, I'll study next semester.' But the time comes and you realize that if you stop working you don't get money. You have to keep working and you have to put off your studies."

—Leonardo, 24 years old, participates in Dirección Nacional de Juventud (DINAJU) Project, province of Buenos Aires

Education is a basic human right, an entitlement of every citizen. A good in itself, education is also a means to raise welfare. Human capital shapes the path for young people's transition to adulthood—to become productive and globally competitive workers, responsive and caring parents, and informed citizens and community leaders. Early school leaving, often for reasons beyond young people's control, may limit opportunities and lead to permanently lower welfare and limited learning over the lifecycle. Education is also key to breaking the intergenerational cycle of poverty—and it protects against many other risks that can hinder young people's transition to adulthood. However, in Argentina 48 percent of the youth age cohort (20–24) do not finish secondary education (Census 2001).

The costs of school dropout and low educational attainment are huge for the individual and for the Argentine society. The economy is less efficient as a result of foregone investment in youth. Education's positive externalities mean that the economy may end up in a suboptimal equilibrium. Inequality will grow if resources are allocated by ability to pay rather than by ability to learn.

Overall, Argentina's youth are well educated, but successfully integrating the poor and the marginal remains a challenge to becoming more competitive globally. Human capital is nurtured early in life, first at home, then in child care, preschool, and primary school. As the global wave of economic and technological change demands more from workers, more and more children continue to secondary school. Higher levels of education can protect against the negative impacts of economic cycles (Chapter 4). The government of Argentina has identified the noncompletion of high school as the principal educational deficit, passing a new education law mandating completion of secondary education.

Early school dropout can contribute to many risky behaviors (see Table 1.2): early entry into the labor market,[11] drinking, smoking, drug use, risky sex, and involvement in crime or violence. Attending school, conversely, helps youth avoid these risks. Staying in school also makes youth more likely to participate in society: to vote and participates in politics, play sports, and engage in clubs and cultural activities. Yet, a significant number of young people in Argentina abandon their educations and drop out of school (Kit and Giovagnoli 2005). To find ways to improve young people's chances of completing secondary education, this chapter addresses the state of education in Argentina and analyzes the links between educational outcomes and individual and school characteristics. It focuses on aspects of secondary education: education attainment and quality, school progression and risk factors, and the likelihood of starting and completing secondary education.[12]

High Enrollments, but Challenges for the Poor

Many Argentines are well educated, with an advanced education system compared with most of Latin America. Youth literacy rates are high, among the highest in the region. Only 1.6 percent of young men and 1.1 percent of young women were illiterate in 2003 (Table 3.1). Primary education is nearly universal and secondary enrollment rates are close to those of the United States. Tertiary enrollment is the highest in the region, in line with that of France.

Net secondary enrollment rates have increased impressively at all levels during 1992–2005—from 65 percent in 1992 to 83 percent in 2005—especially for young men (Table 3.2). Moreover, net enrollment rates increased for all quintiles, but more so for the median than for the top or bottom quintiles.

Enrollment growth has outpaced population growth for all age groups since the early 1980s (Table 3.3). In 1991–2001 enrollment growth was 33 percentage points higher than population growth for young people ages 15–17. The educational system proved responsive to the increasing demand. In 2004, 9.9 million students were enrolled in kindergarten, primary, and secondary school in Argentina, the majority (74 percent) in public schools.

Preschool attendance exploded in 1992–2005, reaching 64 percent (Table 3.4). Early schooling and childhood development is key for youth, but 36 percent of urban 3–5-year-olds

---

11. This refers to "pull factors" such as immediate cash. It could also reflect parental shortsightedness if they "push" their children into the labor force.

12. The educational system in Argentina originates in the National Constitution of 1853, which established the right to teach and learn. An important administrative reform in 1978 transferred national primary schools to the provinces. A new reform program was launched in the early 1990s. First, it transferred national responsibilities for teacher training and secondary (including technical education) and tertiary education to the provinces. Second, it extended mandatory education from 7 years to 10 years. Third, it introduced curricular reform to create one year of preschool, nine years of basic education, and three years of polymodal education. Fourth, it expanded administrative reforms. Finally, it reformed higher education. More recently a new national education law (law 26.206, December 2006) modified the structure of educational levels, which are once again called primary and secondary education, and extended mandatory education to the end of secondary school. The latter includes a basic cycle and a guided cycle. These reforms will be implemented within five years.

Table 3.1. Education Indicators in Latin America and the Caribbean and the OECD

Country	Youth Illiteracy in 2003 (percent)		Secondary Enrollment in 2001–02 (percent)		Tertiary Enrollment in 2000–01 (percent)	
	Male	Female	Male	Female	Male	Female
Argentina	1.6	1.1	79	83	45.4	67.4
Bolivia	1.6	5.3	68[a]	67[a]	40.0	21.8
Brazil	5.3	3.1	69	74	15.9	20.6
Chile	1.1	0.8	73[a]	76[a]	39.1	35.9
Colombia	3.3	2.0	51	56	23.0	25.3
Ecuador	2.1	2.6	50	50	—	—
Mexico	2.2	2.9	59	61	22.0	21.0
Uruguay	1.1	0.5	68	76	26.5	48.1
France	—	—	91[a]	93[a]	48.0	59.0
United States	—	—	85	85	70.0	94.0

Note: a = data for 2000–2001.
Source: Cited in World Bank (2005).

still do not attend preschool (and the percentage is higher in rural areas). Although school enrollment reaches 99 percent for 6–12-year-olds, it falls thereafter, particularly after age 18, dropping to 49 percent for 18–23-year-olds). Net enrollment was up from 74 percent in 1998 to 79 percent in 2003. Females have higher enrollment rates than males and more completed education (Table 3.4).

School nonenrollment has fallen dramatically—by more than 50 percent for 6–17-year-olds in 1980–2001 (Figure 3.1). The risk of youth leaving school, however, increases with age.

Table 3.2. Net Secondary School Enrollment Rates, Selected Years 1992–2005 (percent)

	Total	Gender		Income Quintiles				
		Women	Men	1	2	3	4	5
1992	65	69	60	50	64	60	72	85
1998	79	82	77	66	72	84	90	97
2003	86	88	84	77	84	89	95	97
2003	75	77	72	61	73	75	81	89
2005	83	85	81	71	80	89	93	98

Note: The EPH sample changed in 1998 and again in 2003, therefore two years are included. Only urban areas are included.
Source: CEDLAS.

Table 3.3. Population and Enrollment Growth in 1980, 1991, and 2001

Age Group	1980–1991 (1980 = 100)		1991–2001 (1991 = 100)	
	Population Growth	Enrollment Growth	Population Growth	Enrollment Growth
6–8	117.9	124.5	106.1	107.6
9–11	130.2	132.9	104.2	105.4
12–14	139.5	144.8	100.7	108.7
15–17	125.1	148.5	108.5	141.5

Source: Giovagnoli and Kit (2005). Calculations based on National Population Census.

Table 3.4. Gross Enrollment Rates in Argentina, By Age and Gender, 1992–2005 (percent)

Age	All			Male			Female		
	1992	2000	2005	1992	2000	2005	1992	2000	2005
3–5	34	43	64	34	43	64	35	43	64
6–12	98	99	99	98	99	99	98	99	99
13–17	78	90	91	74	90	90	83	91	92
18–23	41	49	49	38	45	46	45	53	52

Note: 12 cities were included in 1992 and 15 cities in 2000. A different structure was used in 2005 (continuous).
Source: CEDLAS based on EPH.

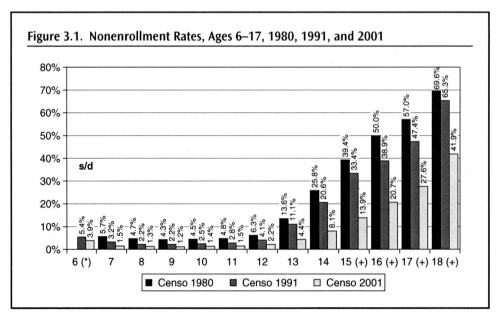

Figure 3.1. Nonenrollment Rates, Ages 6–17, 1980, 1991, and 2001

Source: Kit and Scasso (2006) based on Censo 1980, 1991, and 2001.

Table 3.5. Nonenrollment, By Area, 2001

Area	Population (Ages 6–17)	Teenagers Out of School	Nonenrollment Rates (Percent)
Urban total	7,114,174	423,746	6.0
Rural total	991,720	145,512	14.7
Grouped rural	314,691	28,292	9.0
Dispersed rural	677,029	117,220	17.3
Total	8,105,894	569,258	7.0

Note: Urban population is people living in towns with more than 2,000 inhabitants. Rural population is divided between "grouped" towns smaller than 2,000 and dispersed areas (open countryside).
Source: Censo 2001.

In 1980 the proportion of 14-year-olds not in school (25.8 percent) was the double that of 13-year-olds (13.6 percent). In 2001, 4.4 percent of 13-year-olds did not attend school, but the proportion jumped to 8.1 percent for 14-year-olds and 14 percent for 15-year-olds. Even so, outcomes have improved.

Significant differences remain across geographic areas. Youth in dispersed rural areas are more likely to be out of school—10.3 percent higher than the national average of 7 percent for 6–17-year-olds in 2001 (Table 3.5).[13] Santiago del Estero, Misiones, Tucumán, Chaco, Formosa, and Corrientes are educationally disadvantaged compared with the rest of the country. In Santiago del Estero 16 percent of 6–17-year-olds are out of the formal education system, compared with 8 percent in Santa Fe. The situation is worse for 15–17-year-olds: 45 percent in Santiago are not attending school, 40.7 percent in Tucuman, 39.1 percent in Misiones, and 32.8 percent in Chaco. The National Ministry of Education, Science, and Technology has just launched the Rural Education Improvement Program (Programa de Mejoramiento de la Educación Rural—PROMER) to provide teaching and material support to these schools. The program targets reducing grade repetition and dropout in primary education and expanding secondary education.

Income gaps in enrollment are large. While less than one percent of the 6–17-year-olds from the richest quintile are not in school, this figure rises to 8.2 percent for those in the poorest quintile. Furthermore, young men do worse than young women in the poorer quintiles (Table 3.6). The proportion of young men outside the formal education system is lower than that of females in quintiles 3–5, but young men do worse in the poorest quintiles.

Of youth attending school, almost a third are over-age (below the expected grade for their age). The share of over-age youth increases from 10 percent for 7-year-olds to 44 percent for 17-year-olds (Figure 3.2). The correlation between age-grade distortion and income is

---

13. The federal education law have until recently allowed for differences across provinces in the system of education.

Table 3.6. Nonenrollment and Attendance Rates By Quintile for 6–17-year-olds (percent)

Adult Equivalent Income Quintiles	Nonenrollment			Over-age Attending Students		
	Total	Female	Male	Total	Female	Male
1	8.2	7.9	8.5	35.8	33.3	38.4
2	6.3	5.3	7.1	29.0	26.3	31.7
3	3.7	4.0	3.4	23.5	21.5	25.6
4	1.9	2.4	1.4	18.0	15.2	20.6
5	0.9	0.9	0.8	12.3	10.6	13.9
Total	5.1	4.9	5.2	26.2	23.9	28.4

Note: Adult equivalent income is total household income divided by the total number of equivalent adults.
Source: Calculations from EPH (2000 October wave).

strong (Table 3.6). In the poorest quintile 36 percent of the students ages 6–17 are over-age, compared with only 12 percent in the richest quintile. Age-grade distortion may reflect delayed primary school entry, schooling interruptions, or grade repetition. An inefficient use of resources, excessive grade repetition raises the number of student-years needed to

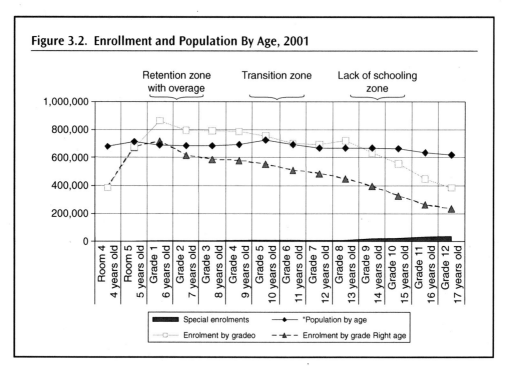

Figure 3.2. Enrollment and Population By Age, 2001

Source: Kit, España, and Labate (2006) based on Censo Nacional de Población (2001) and Relevamiento Anual de Matrícula y Cargos (2001).

produce one graduate and reduces teacher attention for non-over-age students by raising class sizes.

Repetition is common in Argentina, most frequent in grades 1–4. Repetition rates are substantially higher in public than in private schools. Estimated repetition rates for the fourth grade in public schools are more than five times those in private schools (5.5 percent compared with 0.9 percent). And once a public school student repeats a grade the chances to repeat again grow. Repetition—especially during early grades—can affect educational outcomes. Conditional on having completed primary school, repeaters in primary school are less likely than nonrepeaters to enroll in secondary school (64 percent compared with 95 percent). Even for those who start secondary school, the chance of completion is much lower for repeaters (39 percent) than nonrepeaters (70 percent). About 10 percent of students repeat at least the first grade, a sign of inefficiency in Argentina's education system. In Chile less than 3 percent of primary students repeat, in Ecuador 4 percent repeat, and in Scandinavia repetition is close to zero. Repetition is a risk factor for other risky behaviors (chapters 4–6). Repetition falls during the course of primary school. As high as 10 percent for first graders, repetition drops to only 4.3 percent for sixth graders.

Access to school is nearly universal in first grade. Indeed, enrollment is larger than the population under age 10 during the first grades of primary school because students fail and repeat early grades. But an abrupt decrease occurs around age 14, making grades 9–12 the riskiest for school leaving.

High enrollment rates in the last two decades have not translated into equivalent completion rates, though average years of schooling increased by one year over 1992–2005, reaching 10.4 years in 2005 (Table 3.7). Well above the regional average of 5.9 years, Argentina also does well compared with East Asia, where average educational attainment is 7.6 years (Giovagnoli, Fizsbein, and Patrinos 2004; Barro and Lee 2000).

Inequalities in educational attainment—already high—are growing. People from the lowest income quintile complete an average of 7.9 years of education, while those from the highest quintile complete 13.3 years, a gap of nearly 70 percent. And the achievement gap has grown—the increase in attainment did not benefit all income groups equally. The wealthiest three quintiles increased years of schooling by 1–1.2 years, the two poorest by only 0.7–0.8 years.

Table 3.7. **Average Years of Education, By Household Income Quintile, 1992, 2000, and 2005**

	Quintile					
Year	1	2	3	4	5	Mean
1992	7.2	7.8	8.5	9.7	12.2	9.4
2000	7.2	8.2	9.2	10.3	13.2	10.0
2005	7.9	8.6	9.7	11.0	13.3	10.4

Note: 12 cities were included in 1992 and 15 cities in 2000. A different structure (continuous) was used in 2005.
Source: CEDLAS.

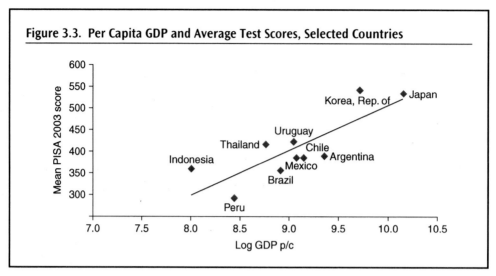

Figure 3.3. Per Capita GDP and Average Test Scores, Selected Countries

Source: Groppelo (2006).

The deficits adolescents bring to secondary education worsen under traditional secondary education, designed to select those able to continue to higher education rather than educate all.[14] The current administration has launched national and provincial plans to change these features, but data for evaluation are not yet available. These efforts target demand, especially through scholarships to low-income students (with 600,000 recipients in 2007). They also target supply through tutoring programs, teacher training, school strengthening, and creating spaces attractive to youth.

Ensuring Quality Remains a Challenge

A solid education system is built on both school quantity and school quality. Access to education and grade attainment are important, but so are test scores and other learning measures. Education helps youth transition to adulthood—but only if they learn the skills they need.

The quality of education in Latin American and the Caribbean is very low. Latin American countries consistently ranked among the lowest in math, reading, science, and problem solving in the OECD's Programme for International Student Assessment (PISA).[15] Even after controlling for per capita GDP, the performance of most of the region is substandard (Figure 3.3; World Bank 2008).

Argentina lags behind the expected test scores for its per capita income (Figure 3.5). In the 2000 PISA Argentina ranked 35 of 41 countries in reading on PISA. Large variation

---

14. This is a holdover from political considerations at the founding of Argentina's educational system. See Tedesco (1982).

15. PISA is the survey of the knowledge and skills of 15-year-old students in reading covering 41 countries, including 15 non-OECD countries.

in test scores due to differences across regions, schools, and student socioeconomic backgrounds drove Argentina's performance (Table 3.8). Argentina and Mexico, for example, have similar average test scores, but Argentina's standard deviation is much larger (World Bank 2006b).

Risk Factors Impede School Progression

Why are youth in Argentina leaving after primary school or dropping out of secondary school—making choices that lower their chances of a successful transition to adulthood? There are different theories: lack of nearby secondary schools (especially in rural areas), the inability of low-income students to pay the opportunity cost of attending school, and irrelevant or outdated curricula lowering school quality. This section explores the interrelations between quantitative educational outcomes and individual and school characteristics, focusing on correlation rather than causation. The analyses are based on the EEJ survey (see Box 1.3) that contains a module specific to young people living in greater Buenos Aires. The survey lack national coverage, and therefore as other EPHs does not cover rural areas. Hence the focus is on the big urban center and cannot be extrapolated to rural and indigenous populations.

Table 3.8. Test Scores for Latin America and the OECD in 2000

Country	Score
Argentina	418
Brazil	396
Chile	410
Mexico	422
Peru	327
OECD	500

Source: World Bank (2006b).

Education is cumulative, so tracking paths is important (Hanushek 1979, 1986). Only 1.6 percent of 15–30-year-olds in greater Buenos Aires never finished primary school, while 9 percent completed primary school but never enrolled in secondary school (Figure 3.4).[16] Of those 24–30 years old, 16 percent never attended secondary school, compared with only 9 percent of those 18–24 (Table 3.9). Of those 15–17 years old, 12 percent have already dropped out of secondary school. These findings, based on greater Buenos Aires, do not apply to rural areas, where many more students never finish primary school and do not enroll in secondary school. Thus, national average figures are likely to be less encouraging.

Youth at greatest risk—those who never attended or never completed secondary school—started working earlier than those who completed secondary school. The average age of entry into secondary school for those who dropped out is one year more than the age of those who finished—14 years compared with 13 years.

Of youth who drop out, 52 percent cited employment as the main reason for leaving.[17] Poor academic performance (16 percent) and pregnancy (8 percent) were also important

---

16. These two subgroups together will be referred to as "never attended," as their progress stopped before entering secondary school. There are three possible outcomes for the group that initiated secondary education: completed secondary, dropped out before completion (not completed), and still attending.

17. EEJ and Sidicaro and Fanfani (1998) found similar results for greater Buenos Aires using a survey from 1995. Binstok and Cerruti (2005) also mention this factor.

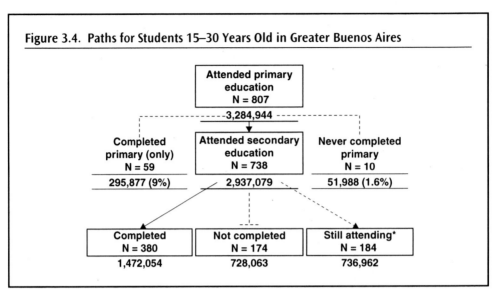

Figure 3.4. Paths for Students 15–30 Years Old in Greater Buenos Aires

Source: Calculations based on EEJ.

(see Chapter 6). Those who never started secondary school cited work, poor academic performance, and family problems as constraints.

Supportive parents are key to youth's educational success. The chance of starting secondary education is 93 percent for youth who felt their parents were very engaged in their education, while the figure drops to 78 percent for those who did not perceive parent interest. The probability of completion is also higher for those who felt supported than for those who did not (73 percent compared with 16 percent).

Better educated mothers take better care of their children and encourage better educational outcomes. Of children whose mothers hold a university degree, 94 percent completed secondary school. Completion decreased to 46 percent for those whose mothers completed only primary school and to a third for those whose mothers have some primary

Table 3.9. Educational Outcomes of Young People, By Age (percent)

Age Group	Completed	Not Completed°	Still Attending	Never Attended
15–17	1.4	11.7	82.8*	4.1
18–24	55.5*	27.2	8.7	8.7
25–30	58.7*	23.4	2.3	15.6
Total	44.8*	22.16*	22.4*	10.6

°And out of the educational system.
*Coefficient of variation less than 10 percent. The rest of the figures have a coefficient of variation above 10 percent.
Source: Calculations based on EEJ.

Table 3.10. Mothers' and Children's Schooling in Greater Buenos Aires in
             2005–Maxium Level of Education Achieved (Transition Matrix) (percent)

Mother/Child	Primary Incomplete	Primary Complete	Secondary Incomplete	Secondary Complete	Tertiary Incomplete	Tertiary Complete
None	35.5	10.7	26.5	13.2	14.1	0.0
Primary incomplete	5.1	20.9	42.5	20.2	9.1	2.2
Primary complete	2.1	18.6	32.6	21.5	18.4	6.8
Secondary incomplete	0.0	5.4	32.3	26.5	27.2	8.6
Secondary complete	0.0	1.6	22.6	18.6	52.1	5.1
Tertiary incomplete	0.0	0.0	4.2	15.2	68.5	12.0
Tertiary complete	0.0	0.0	6.5	7.5	62.5	23.5

Source: Calculations based on EEJ.

education only (Table 3.10).[18] Conversely, no youth whose mothers hold a university degree did not complete primary school. The intergenerational transmission of education is strong.

The Probability of Starting Secondary School

What determines whether a young person starts and completes secondary school? Multivariate analysis is used to estimate adjusted probabilities of starting and completing secondary school, controlling for a range of factors. Family background is shown to have very strong effects, with weaker effects for school variables.

Students who repeated a year between grade 1–3 or 4–7 are less likely to attend secondary school (12 percent for repeaters of grades 1–3, 8 percent for repeaters of grades 4–7). Moreover, repetition effects are cumulative—a student who repeated in both periods is 20 percent less likely to enroll in secondary school than a peer who did not repeat (Table 3.11).[19]

Consistent with previous studies cited, youth whose parents did not complete primary education are 12 percent less likely to enroll in secondary education than those whose parents completed secondary education. So limited access to secondary schooling for this generation will hurt future generations.

Gender is not important in determining secondary school enrollment. Neither is having a tutor during primary school,[20] nor whether youth attend public or private primary school.

_____

18. It excludes those individuals who still attend secondary school.

19. Huber/White/sandwich estimator of variance was used. Estimated marginal probabilities are calculated at means of variables and holding constant other factors in the logit equation.

20. This means that a student had access to private teacher (tutor) during primary school.

Table 3.11. Likelihood of Starting Secondary School, 2005

Variable	Marginal Probability
Repeat grades 1–3	−0.12
Repeat grades 4–7	−0.08
Male	0.00
Parent not educated	−0.15
Parent with some primary education only	−0.12
Parent with some secondary education only	−0.04
Books	0.01
Worked before age 13	−0.03
Private teacher or tutor	0.00
Public school	−0.02
Simple school	0.00
Urban school	−0.01
Cohort 1981–85	−0.03
Cohort 1975–80 Constant	−0.04

Logit Model; Sample size: 797. The keys for policymakers are the marginal probabilities. These indicate the chance of starting secondary school for a student with specific characteristics. For example, a student who repeated in grades 1–3 has a 12 percent lower chance of starting secondary school than peers who did not repeat in grades 1–3.
Source: Calculations based on EEJ.

The Probability of Completing Secondary School

The probability of completing secondary school is correlated with the level of parents' education, repetition in primary school, gender, and textbook availability (Table 3.12).[21] Grade repetition in primary school is strongly correlated with the probability of completing secondary school, even after taking into account other individual and school factors. Young men are significantly less likely than young women to complete secondary school. Interestingly, the chances of completing secondary school are higher for older cohorts. Those born in 1975–80 are more likely to finish than those born in 1986–1990. This may reflect worsening macroeconomic conditions affecting young people's school–work decisions (see Chapter 4).

Students with textbooks have a 16 percent higher chance of finishing secondary school than peers without books. Scholarship availability does not seem to affect completion significantly. This may be because of the small number of people in the sample receiving a scholarship. Students in private secondary schools do better— those in religious private schools are 14 percent more likely to finish secondary school than their public school peers.

Student Profiles and Secondary School Completion

Youth with textbooks who did not repeat any grade during primary school and whose parents completed secondary school have an 88 percent chance of completing secondary school, 11.5 percentage points above the average (Table 3.13). The probability of completing secondary school falls 16 percentage points for youth who repeated in primary school but have otherwise similar characteristics. Adding the effect of not having textbooks during secondary school drops their chances to 54 percent. Youth with no textbooks who

---

21. Huber/White/sandwich estimator of variance was used.

repeated in primary school and whose parents have only a primary school degree have a 30 percent chance of completing secondary school.

When young people spend more time in school they are less likely to commit a crime (Wolfe 1995). Higher educational attainment also reduces the incidence of risky sexual behavior and drug and alcohol use (Chapters 5 and 6). So high risk groups need special attention and support to increase their chances of completing secondary school.

Table 3.12. Likelihood of Completing Secondary School, 2005

Variable	Marginal Probability
Repeat grades 1–3	−0.22
Repeat grades 4–7	−0.23
Male	−0.09
Parent uneducated	−0.31
Parent with some primary education only	−0.26
Parent with some secondary education only	−0.19
Books	0.16
Worked before 13	−0.17
Scholarship	−0.02
Same school	−0.08
Private religious	0.14
Private nonreligious	0.12
School with languages	0.11
Simple school	0.01
Urban school	−0.09
Public school	−0.12
Cohort 1981–85	0.10
Cohort 1975–80	0.17
Constant	

Note: Logit model; Sample size: 554. The keys for policymakers are the marginal probabilities. These indicate the chance of completing secondary school for a student with specific characteristics. For example, a student that repeated in grades 1–3 has a 22 percent lower chance of completing secondary school than his\her peers that did not repeat in grades 1–3.
Source: Calculations based on EEJ.

Table 3.13. Is a Student Likely to Complete Secondary School?

Repeated Primary School	No	Yes	Yes	Yes
Textbooks	Yes	Yes	No	No
Parent with some secondary education only	No	No	No	Yes
Parent has more than secondary education	Yes	Yes	Yes	No
Pr(y = 1|x)	0.88	0.72	0.54	0.30
Confidence Intervals	0.83,0.92	0.57,0.87	0.31,0.76	0.12,0.48

Note: Data are for 2005. Confidence intervals by delta method.
Source: Calculations based on EEJ.

Challenges in Expanding Education for the Poor and Marginal

"The situation of young people from the working-class neighborhoods where I work in Corrientes: most of them do odd jobs, cut grass, do cleaning, work in construction, work as street vendors, and all with schooling or even minimum training. The first problem they face is whether to work or study, because they have to help feed their families and it's very hard for them to study or get training."

—Nelson, 22 years old; works in a grassroots organization, Corrientes.

Argentina has made great progress since the 1980s. Illiteracy has been virtually eradicated among today's youth, and enrollment in primary education is nearly universal. The government has managed to maintain high enrollment through difficult times: the largest youth cohort ever in a period of significant macroeconomic swings. However, challenges remain: significant differences in educational outcomes persist by wealth and location. While less than 1 percent of 6–17-year-olds from the richest 20 percent of households are not in school, this number rises to 8.2 percent for those from the poorest 20 percent of households. Children and youth in rural areas have a higher probability of dropping out than those in urban areas and few possibilities to continue studying in the area where they live.

Student, family, and school characteristics affect young people's chances of enrolling secondary school—and their chances of graduating. Students who repeated a grade in primary school are less likely to attend secondary school. And multiple repeats lower their chances even further. High risk groups need special attention and support to offset disadvantages.

Some of the most pressing issues for consideration and discussion are summed up in the following:

- What is the best strategy to reduce repetition, increase completion rates, and improve educational quality in primary school? How can poor performers be detected and how can remedial support be ensured?
- What is the most efficient strategy to increase enrollment, improve quality, and raise completion rates in secondary school? How can a focus on the poorest areas be ensured in the expansion and improvement of secondary education?
- How can the growing gap in attainment between poor and nonpoor youth be addressed most effectively?
- How can a focus on at-risk youth be ensured in order to create positive intergenerational effects?
- How can parent engagement be increased to encourage youth enrollment and completion?
- How can the school environment be used to provide key prevention messages to the "captive audience" of the youth cohort?

CHAPTER 4

Labor Markets and Business Cycles

By Roxana Maurizio, Dorte Verner, and Michael Justesen

"I represent a group of young people from the outlying suburbs who work because they have to help their families. In many cases, these are families where the parents are separated and the young people are taking care of their families. It's like switching roles. Young people don't do work that they like. They work because they have to in order to survive."

—Susana, 23 years old, Posadas

The labor market is critical for youth as a place to earn income and accumulate skills after leaving school. But unemployment deprives them of these benefits, lowering labor force participation and raising adult unemployment (World Bank 2008). Unemployment may also lead to depression and other health issues and has been identified by some as a risk factor for violence.

Some Argentine young people start working at age 15, while others wait until their early twenties. In either case they expect to reap the benefits of investments in education and health. An important mark of independence, the transition to the workforce is also difficult and costly. Periods of inactivity or unemployment prevent the accumulation of human capital, job skills, and a positive employment history—keys for job seeking (World Bank 2006b).

Today's youth are better educated than older generations, but unemployment rates for youth in Argentina are much higher than those for adults, and the trend is getting worse. Economic theory predicts that increased educational attainment will ease the transition to work and bring greater job success. Some youth have benefited, but others still face challenges in finding work—even though returns to secondary and higher education have increased for both youth and adults.

A new feature has emerged in the social landscape in the past two decades: youth who neither study nor work, or who work in precarious, low-skill jobs without qualifications.

The exclusion of these young people stems partly from their unemployment and poverty but partly from society's stereotypes linking them to crime, violence, drugs, and idleness. Projected through media and politics, these representations make it more difficult for youth to participate in society (Chapter 7).[22]

For decades entry into the labor market organized the transition to adulthood. The transition from school to the labor market, however, has become a bottleneck for a large share of young people. A recent survey indicates that 50–55 percent of people ages 18–24 from low-income households had no jobs or worked only occasionally during the year of the survey (Fundación Banco de la Provincia de Buenos Aires 2005).

This chapter analyzes the relations among growth, business cycles, and youth labor market outcomes (wage returns, unemployment, and occupational mobility). The chapter begins by documenting employment, unemployment, and wages for youth in Argentina. The next section addresses labor market wage returns and the likelihood of unemployment during business cycles. The last section discusses occupational mobility.[23] The chapter concludes with some questions to guide policy debates.

Difficult Times for Youth in Employment, Unemployment, and Wages

> "Where I come from, where not everybody is in the same situation as I am, people work because they need to, people work because they have to, and they're exploited, and they're paid under the table, but it's an obligation."
>
> —Pablo, 19 years old, participates in a grassroots organization and works, Formosa

Many Argentines start to work very young, with severe consequences for later life. In Argentina 8.6 percent of 7–14-year-olds work exclusively, which is high compared with Chile (4 percent). Those who sacrifice schooling when young are more likely to be poor as adults, their productivity reduced by a lack of accumulated human capital and skills (World Bank 2006b). Early labor market entry is associated with a number of risky behaviors (Table 1.2), including unsafe sexual activities and alcohol and tobacco use. Staying in school reduces the likelihood of engaging in these behaviors, in addition to increasing wages and reducing unemployment.

Employment

The Argentine labor market—with its protections for individual workers, high barriers to dismissal, and large fringe benefits—is attractive for young workers but difficult for them to enter successfully. Employers are reluctant to hire when it is difficult to fire, placing youth at a disadvantage (Table 4.1). Employment has risen for older workers, but the proportion of young workers has fallen from 21 percent to 18 percent over 1992–2005.

---

22. Exclusion hits rural youth (about 9 percent of the youth population) particularly hard (Roman 2003 Almost invisible, not only in Argentina but also throughout the continent, rural youth often remain at the margins of both family structures and national policies (Durston 1997, 1998).

23. Most of the analysis in this chapter is for 1992–2003 and based on EPH.

Table 4.1. Age Distribution of Employed Workers, 1992, 2000, and 2005 (percent)

	0–14	15–24	25–40	41–64	65+
1992	1.1	21.0	36.5	38.6	2.9
2000	0.3	19.0	37.7	39.8	3.2
2005	0.5	17.7	37.1	40.6	4.1

Note: 12 cities included in 1992, 15 cities in 2000. 2005 has a different structure (continuous).
Source: CEDLAS.

The share of female employees in the workforce has increased in the last decade. In 2005, 45 percent of employed workers were women, up 5 percentage points since 1992. The female share is lower partly because women stay in school longer and partly because women do most of the childrearing. Unemployment rates are also higher for women.

Youth are working fewer hours than in the early 1990s, a trend particularly evident among low-skilled workers (World Bank 2005a). This decline suggests that youth, especially the unskilled, are more likely to find part-time, less stable jobs. The economic downturn reduced average hours worked for all age groups, but it hit the young hardest.

Among the youngest workers (those 15–19), many do not attend school and live in poor households—they left school to look for a job to supplement low household earnings. The very low educational levels these individuals attain will not be enough to escape the poverty trap, transmitting poverty across generations.

Unemployment

Youth unemployment rates in the region are twice those of other workers. In Argentina they are three times as high (Figure 4.1).[24] Economic changes made matters worse, raising the gap between younger and older workers from about 8 percent in 1992 to 21 percent in 2003. Service-oriented sectors drove growth in the 1990s, demanding higher skilled workers generally over 24 years of age (World Bank 2005a). In contrast, the recent recovery has been driven mainly by manufacturing, requiring less skilled workers.

Youth unemployment increased by 25 percentage points in Argentina over 1992–2002, though since then it has fallen dramatically (Figures 4.2 and 4.3). Even during the strong growth of the early 1990s youth unemployment proliferated, reaching 38.8 percent in 2002—far higher than in Brazil (20.5 in 2001) and Mexico (7.2 percent in 2002).[25] In contrast, adult unemployment rose to about 20 percent.[26]

24. See, for example, Cacciamali (2005); Justesen and Verner (2006); and World Bank (2003). Similarly, the YSCS data suggest that about 22 percent of youth are unemployed, compared with 7 percent of the adult population.

25. In Brazil and Chile youth entering the labor market during recessions experience atypically high unemployment, even after recovery begins (World Bank 2006b).

26. Youth unemployment tends to be higher in urban areas. Because only urban areas are covered by the data used in this chapter, unemployment rates are reported as an upper limit (World Bank 2006b). Even before the crisis in 2001, when the Youth Training Programs were in place, the chances of finding employment after participating in the programs were slim (35 percent) (see Victor Elis and others 2004).

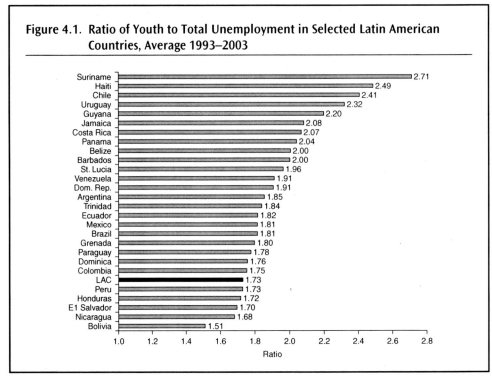

Figure 4.1. Ratio of Youth to Total Unemployment in Selected Latin American Countries, Average 1993–2003

Source: Regional Youth Study (World Bank forthcoming).

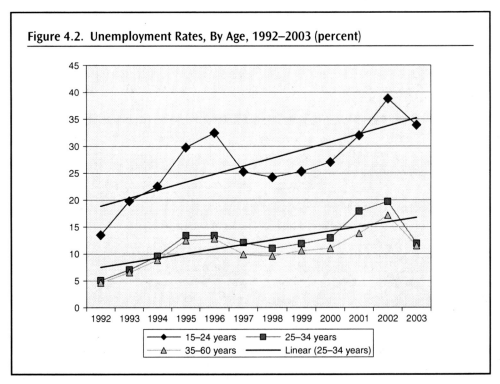

Figure 4.2. Unemployment Rates, By Age, 1992–2003 (percent)

Source: Calculations based on EPH.

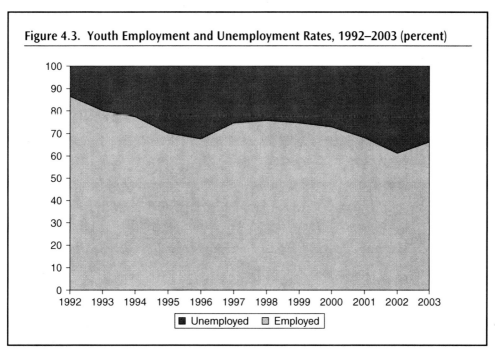

Figure 4.3. Youth Employment and Unemployment Rates, 1992–2003 (percent)

Source: Calculations based on EPH.

Poor households have more unemployment and less employment than nonpoor households, especially for young adults between the ages of 24 and 29 (less for younger cohorts; Figure 4.4). Entering the labor market earlier, men outnumber women as market participants (Figure 4.5). Unemployment, however, is relatively equal for men and women as a proportion of all youth (not only labor market participants), indicating that young women have higher joblessness despite higher average education.

Unemployment duration and job search time for the unemployed have also increased (Table 4.2). Youth unemployment duration increased by 111 percent (to 9.8 months) over 1992–2005, compared with a larger increase of 190 percent for older workers (to 10.7 months). Long periods of unemployment are especially costly for youth, discouraging them from remaining in the labor force and preventing them from building their skills. Moreover, long-term youth unemployment can increase poverty-youth wages are often important parts of household income.

Wages

Older workers (ages 45–54) earn nearly double the hourly wages of young workers. Youth wages fell from 64 percent of adult wages in 1992 to just 57 percent in 2003—a trend correlated with unemployment. But more and better schooling helps. Although youth still earn far lower wages than adults, youth with tertiary education received 8 percent higher wages than secondary graduates in 1992 but 32 percent higher wages in 2003.

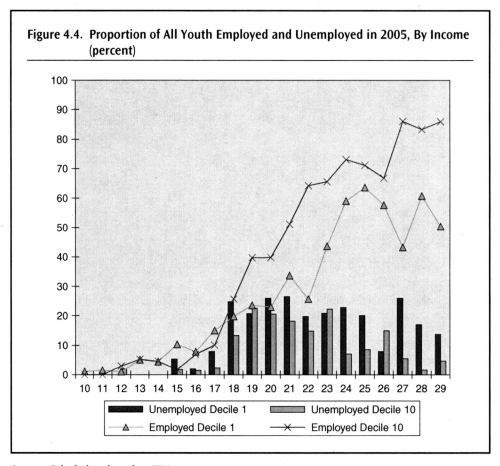

Figure 4.4. Proportion of All Youth Employed and Unemployed in 2005, By Income (percent)

Source: Calculations based on EPH.

Higher educational attainment raises hourly wages (Figure 4.6). Workers with tertiary education earned 82 percent more than workers with secondary education only, 167 percent more than workers with primary education only, and 197 percent more than workers with no education in 1992–2003. Wage workers with secondary education earned 47 more than workers with primary education only and 63 percent more than workers with no education. Workers with primary education earned 11 percent more than uneducated workers. Although real wages for workers with tertiary education dropped the most in nominal terms, their relative wages dropped the least. Those completing secondary education (but not tertiary) had the largest relative drop in real wages.

With youth concentrated in industries with larger reductions in protections and a larger proportion of low-skilled workers, trade liberalization may have decreased their wages relative to those of other workers. The increase in wage inequality since the 1990s supports this possibility (World Bank 2005a). Youth real wages fell 38 percent between 1992 and 2003, compared with 22 percent for older workers (Figure 4.7). Across Argentina real hourly wages of youth have fallen against those of older workers, with relative wages lower in the Northwest and slightly higher in Pampeana (Figure 4.8).

Figure 4.5. **Proportion of All Youth Employed and Unemployed in 2005, By Gender (percent)**

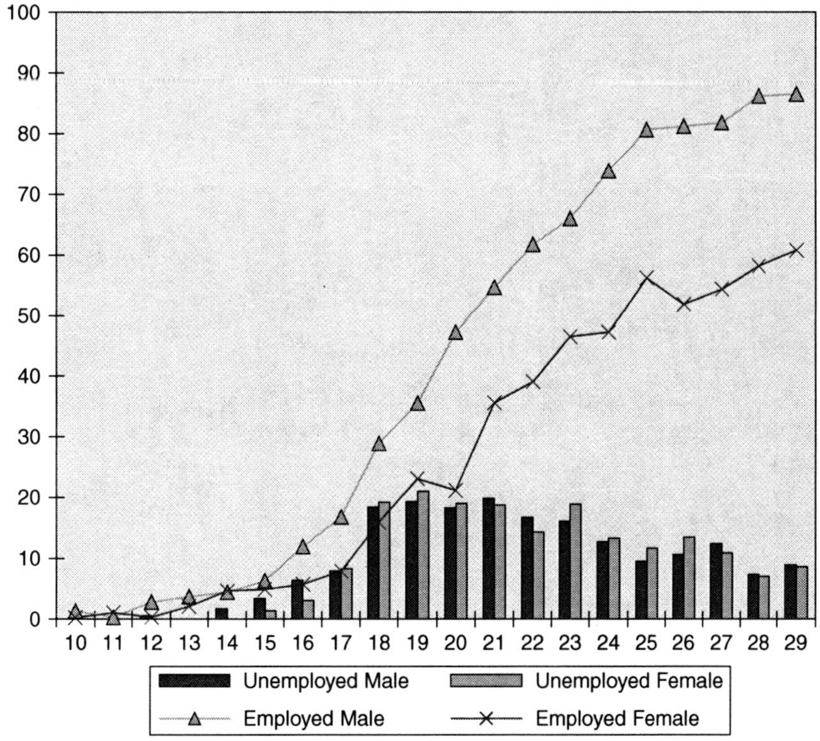

Source: Calculations based on EPH.

Youth Fared Badly During Business Cycles

"For me, work is hard to get because for young people, and for me, you have to be over-qualified to get a job. For unskilled work they are requiring a high school diploma, even university, and this doesn't make any sense. That leaves out kids who for one reason or another couldn't finish high school."

—Natalia, 20 years old, province of Buenos Aires.

Table 4.2. **Duration of Unemployment (months)**

Year	Total	Age		
		15–24	25–64	65+
1992	3.8	4.0	3.7	4.3
2000	6.6	6.3	6.8	6.0
2005	9.8	8.4	10.7	11.4

Note: 12 cities included in 1992, 15 cities in 2000; 2005 has a different structure (continuous).
Source: CEDLAS.

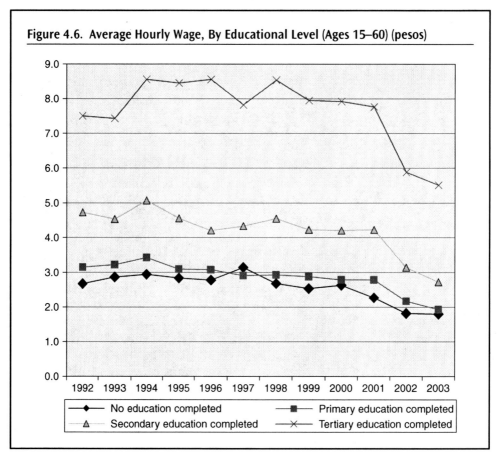

Figure 4.6. Average Hourly Wage, By Educational Level (Ages 15–60) (pesos)

Source: Calculations based on EPH.

By examining data from 1992–2003 this section analyzes how youth wage returns and unemployment rates at different levels of schooling have changed and compares these returns and unemployment rates with those of adults to determine how economic fluctuations affected the labor market. It finds that youth labor market outcomes are affected by general trends in poverty and economic growth.

Youth benefit disproportionately from expanding labor markets. Cross-country analyses from developed and developing countries show that increased labor demand increases youth employment and labor market participation (World Bank 2006b). Research on unemployment exit in greater Buenos Aires over 1995–2003 shows that the probability of leaving unemployment is higher when the economy is growing, accounting for business cycle effects and duration dependence (Cerimedo 2004). The same research shows that men have a higher probability than women of leaving unemployment and youth have a higher probability than older workers.

The connections among wage returns, education, and age are analyzed using a panel dataset of household surveys containing 887,536 individuals in all major urban areas in Argentina, covering 1992–2003. While the analysis assesses both long-run and business cycle trends, this section focuses on the effects of business cycles.

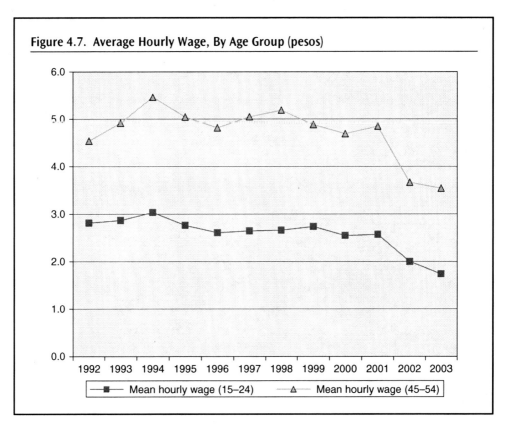

Figure 4.7. Average Hourly Wage, By Age Group (pesos)

Legend: —■— Mean hourly wage (15–24)   ⋯△⋯ Mean hourly wage (45–54)

Source: Calculations based on EPH.

Location matters for long-run wages. Workers in Patagonia and greater Buenos Aires earn higher hourly wages than those in the Cuyo, Northwest, and Pampeana regions. This may reflect larger capital input and financial centers in greater Buenos Aires. Regions such as the mountainous Northwest are sparsely populated, with fewer resources and lower investment inflows.[27] Workers in greater Buenos Aires, however, are also more likely to become unemployed than workers in other regions. Despite the relatively low wages of workers in Cuyo, they are the least likely to be unemployed. With high wages and low unemployment, Patagonia is the best location for workers in Argentina.

Wage returns rose as output grew strongly in the early 1990s (particularly 1992–94), but unemployment also increased (Figure 4.4). Wage returns grew slightly more for adults than for youth at all levels of education. Returns to tertiary education grew by 21.3 percent for youth and 25.8 percent for adults, double those to primary education (11.5 percent for youth and 11.9 percent for adults). High education protected youth from some of the effects of rising unemployment. The likelihood of unemployment decreased by 2.7 percent for youth with tertiary education, but grew 50.1 percent for youth with secondary education. The likelihood of unemployment for adults with tertiary education increased 7 percent, compared with an 82.3 percent increase for those with secondary education.

---

27. Wages have not been adjusted for purchasing power parity. So, the higher wages in greater Buenos Aires may reflect a higher cost of living.

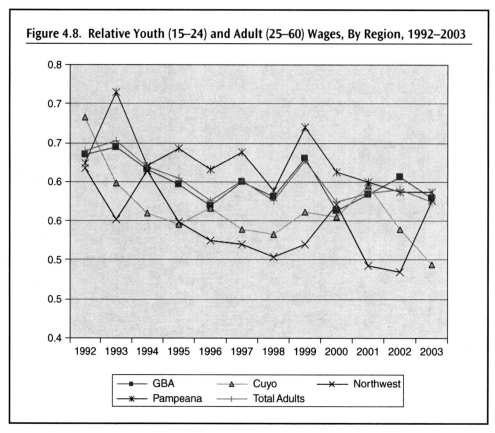

Figure 4.8. Relative Youth (15–24) and Adult (25–60) Wages, By Region, 1992–2003

Source: Calculations based on EPH.

In response to the 1995 tequila crisis[28] unemployment increased and wage returns fell for all educational groups, but especially for young primary and secondary school graduates. The shock reduced wage returns more for youth than adults, except for youth with tertiary education, to this point protected by their high attainment (Table 4.3). The tequila crisis hit the wages of primary school graduates the hardest—a decline of 15 percent in one year. Youth with tertiary education did better than their peers, with a 36 percent increase in unemployment, compared with 44.9 percent for primary-educated youth and an even larger 61.3 percent for secondary-educated youth.

During the slow GDP growth of 1996–98, wage returns continued to fall (for all workers except tertiary-educated adults). Unemployment fell slightly, but less for primary-educated youth, whose wages again dropped the most (13 percent). For all levels of education wages suffered more and unemployment decreased less for youth than adults. Between 1995 and 1998 wage returns fell by 9.3 percent for tertiary-educated youth but remained stable for

---

28. The 1994 economic crisis in Mexico, widely known as the Mexican peso crisis, was triggered by the sudden devaluation of the Mexican peso and spilled over to other countries, including Brazil and Argentina, in 1994–95. In the southern cone and Brazil, the impact that the Mexican economic crisis had on the region was labeled the Tequila crisis

Table 4.3. Change in Wage Returns over Business Cycles (percent)

Years Cycle		1992–1994 Growth	1995 Tequila Crisis	1996–1998 Slow Growth	1999–2002 Collapse	2003 Recovery
Primary	Youth	11.5	−14.8	−13.1	−61.1	3.6
	Adults	11.9	−8.1	−10.4	−48.8	−15.2
Secondary	Youth	17.0	−13.2	−10.5	−41.0	−26.3
	Adults	17.7	−12.9	−5.5	−39.4	−19.8
Tertiary	Youth	21.3	−0.2	−9.3	−51.9	−12.7
	Adults	25.8	−4.7	0.0	−31.7	−16.6

Note: Changes in wage returns are based on conditional wage regression estimates of a pseudo panel data set from 1992–2003 (see appendix IV, table IVA.2).
Source: Calculations based on EPH.

adults with similar education. Unemployment retreated more quickly for tertiary-educated youth than for their less-educated peers (Table 4.4).

The 1999–2002 crisis increased unemployment dramatically and slashed wage returns. Primary-educated youth again lost the most—wage returns declined a staggering 61 percent on top of previous losses (Table 4.3). Wages also fell severely for youth with secondary education (41 percent) and tertiary education (51 percent). The wages of adults at all levels of education declined less. This crisis differed, however, from previous downturns, with unemployment growing faster for adults and more educated youth (Table 4.4).

In 2003 growth resumed and unemployment dropped. Wages, however, continued to fall for all age and education groups (except for primary-educated youth, possibly because manufacturing drove the recovery). Wages for tertiary-educated youth fell less than those

Table 4.4. Change in Likelihood of Being Unemployed over the Business Cycle (percent)

Years Cycle		1992–1994 Growth	1995 Tequila Crisis	1996–1998 Slow Growth	1999–2002 Collapse	2003 Recovery
Primary	Youth	3.91	44.9	−23.0	95.3	−26.4
	Adults	207.1	521.0	−50.2	342.6	−56.5
Secondary	Youth	50.1	61.3	−34.3	137.1	−23.0
	Adults	82.3	626.4	−59.3	915.9	−48.3
Tertiary	Youth	−2.7	36.0	−49.1	290.0	−8.6
	Adults	7.0	98.5	−5100.2	277.0	−92.7

Note: The changes in likelihood of being unemployed are based on conditional probit regression estimates of a pseudo panel dataset from 1992–2003 (see appendix IV, table IVA.2).
Source: Calculations based on EPH.

of adults, 12.7 percent compared with 16.6 percent. Growth reduced unemployment for all age groups and education levels.

These findings suggest that youth are a buffer during recessions, with the wider fluctuations in their wages absorbing the brunt of the blow. These results are consistent with findings from OECD countries—macroeconomic shocks affect youth wages more than those of adults, but unemployment shocks affect adults more than youth (Jimeno and Rodriguez-Palenzuela 2002). Examining 1992–2002 as a whole, wages of primary-educated youth suffered more than those of primary-educated adults and youth with secondary and tertiary education. In general, wage returns and unemployment for tertiary-educated youth performed better, improving more during upturns and deteriorating less during downturns. Secondary-educated youth and adults faced the most difficulties, perhaps reflecting excess supply and skill mismatches. Adults benefited more than youth from the most recent upturns.

Higher Occupational Mobility for Youth

This section analyzes why young Argentine workers face higher risks of leaving their jobs. Occupational instability (transitions into and out of employment and between different jobs) affects household well-being. Increased instability (especially when accompanied by unemployment) often lowers well-being by creating uncertainty about future income, a situation particularly difficult for low-income families. And frequent rotation among different jobs-with or without unemployment—may be associated with low (or no) social security coverage. Moreover, high occupational instability can stop workers from acquiring job skills, particularly harmful for youth who left school early to work.

As unemployment grew and the incidence of precarious employment[29] rose after 1992, occupational instability increased, stimulated by growing unregistered employment and changing labor regulations (the trial period and new types of fixed-term, lower-cost contracts).[30]

Youth and women have higher chances of leaving a job for another position, for unemployment, or for inactivity. Due partly to the prevalence among these groups of informal jobs not registered in the social security system (and so lower firing costs) and partly to a tendency to exit and reenter the labor force, high occupational instability promotes cycles of unemployment, inactivity, and precarious employment.

International research shows that job separation declines with labor market experience and job tenure—the longer workers spend in a job, the less likely they are to leave (negative duration dependence) (Farber 1999; Haile 2004; Leighton and Mincer 1982). Job hazard rates typically differ across demographic groups, with instability highest among women, the less educated, and the young.[31] A study of less educated young workers in the

---

29. Precarious occupations are defined as those held by wage earners not registered in social security.

30. Hopenhayn (2001) analyzed the effects of regulations on instability in Argentina. Similar studies for other countries can be found in Saavedra and Torero (2000) for Peru, in Kugler (2000) for Colombia, and in Calderón-Madrid (2000) for Mexico.

31. See, for example, Parsons (1986) and Farber (1999) on the United States and Haile (2004) on Germany.

United States indicates that employment instability declines with age and with employment experience (Holzer and LaLonde 1998). In Argentina there have been only a few studies of labor market dynamics and none of youth occupational instability.[32] This limited literature suggests that both unemployment and employment have negative duration dependence and that young workers are particularly vulnerable.

To address these issues, data from the Permanent Household Survey (EPH) are analyzed. Although not longitudinal, the survey interviewed households on four successive occasions, each separated by five to seven months. Comparing the situation of an individual on successive occasions highlights changes in occupational status.[33] Hazard function estimates are taken for young workers and compared with those for other workers, controlling for individual and job characteristics. The analysis first looks at changes from one job to any other state—another job, unemployment, or inactivity—before examining state-specific outcomes.

Occupational Mobility of Young Workers

To study the occupational paths followed by youth in the Argentine labor market paths and compare them with those of adult workers, a typology is constructed using information from four successive observations. Mutually exclusive paths are identified, distinguishing both worker state (employment, unemployment, or inactivity) and occupational category (registered, nonregistered, or nonwage; Box 4.1).

Paths 1–3 incorporate those whose state did not change during the four observations (Box 4.1). Path 4 includes those who left an occupation or inactivity and remained unemployed until the last observation. Those observed three times in any state are classified in paths 5–7. Paths 8–10 group individuals who alternated between two states from one interview to another (not remaining in the same state for more than six months). Path 11 includes those who left unemployment or inactivity and remained employed until the last observation.

During the year and a half under observation, path 3 (always inactive) is the most frequent among youth at 33 percent (Table 4.5). For adults, path 1 (always employed) predominates at 50 percent. With only 18 percent always employed, youth have a lower attachment to the labor market (associated with noneconomic activities such as school). Youth also change more often between labor participation and inactivity (paths 9 and 10).

Due to the brief unemployment periods in Argentina for both youth and adults only a few remained unemployed throughout the four interviews (0.9 percent of youth and 0.7 percent of adults; Table 4.5).[34] Considering only those always in the labor force, 80 percent

---

32. Beccaria and Maurizio (2004) analyze the case of greater Buenos Aires and find negative duration dependence. Galiani and Hopenhayn (2000) estimate the risk of unemployment and its distribution, taking into account reincidence of unemployment. They conclude that the total time an individual spends unemployed during a two-year period is close to the high figures found in Europe, especially for youth with incomplete primary education. See also Light and Ureta (1992) and Kupets (2005) for Ukraine.

33. Due to data availability, the analysis focuses on 1995–2003 for 28 main urban centers in Argentina. In 2003 the EPH underwent methodological changes and started publishing quarterly results. The last information available obtained with the traditional methodology is for May 2003.

34. Moreover, the share of cases not classified is higher among youth (14 percent) than adults (8 percent), indicating that the former are more unstable in the labor market.

Box 4.1: Typology of Labor Market Paths

1.	Always employed
1a.	Always employed as wage earner in social security (registered)
1b.	Always employed as wage earner in social security (nonregistered)
1c.	Always employed as nonwage earner
2.	Always unemployed
3.	Always inactive
4.	Enters unemployment and remains unemployed
4a.	Leaves employment as nonregistered wage earner and remains unemployed
4b.	Leaves employment as registered wage earner and remains unemployed
5.	Mainly unemployed (three times observed unemployed, except those classified in path 4)
6.	Mainly inactive (three times observed inactive)
7.	Mainly employed (three times observed employed)
8.	High instability between employment and unemployment
8a.	High instability between employment as nonregistered wage earner and unemployment
8b.	High instability between employment as registered wage earner and unemployment
8c.	High instability between employment as nonwage earner and unemployment
9.	High instability between employment and inactivity
9a.	High instability between employment as nonregistered wage earner and inactivity
9b.	High instability between employment as registered wage earner and inactivity
9c.	High instability between employment as nonwage earner and inactivity
10.	High instability between unemployment and inactivity
11.	Leaves unemployment or inactivity and remains employed
12.	Nonclassified paths

Source: Methodology developed for this report.

of adults were always employed while only 59 percent of youth were always employed (consistent with the higher frequencies of youth in paths 2, 4, and 5). Given the prevalence of nonregistered employment and the high youth occupational instability, youth also registered higher frequencies in path 8, implying transitions between employment (whether registered or nonregistered) and unemployment.[35]

To analyze the occupation mobility of youth, duration models are applied to estimate a hazard function.[36] Several model specifications are used: duration dependence is analyzed through the shape of the baseline hazard, heterogeneity is incorporated to

---

35. Capellari and Jenkins (2002) find similar results for the United States for the determinants of low income, controlling for initial conditions and attrition.

36. The hazard function indicates the probability of ending an episode immediately after time *t*, conditional on the fact that the episode has not yet finished at that moment.

Table 4.5. Paths Followed by Youth and Adult Workers in the Labor Market, 1995–2003 (percent)

Path	Youth	Youth at Least Once in the Labor Force	Youth Always in the Labor Force	Adults	Adults at Least Once in the Labor Force	Adults Always in the Labor Force
1	18.2	27.2	58.8	49.9	60.3	79.7
1a	6.9	10.3	22.3	23.3	28.2	37.2
1b	3.1	4.7	10.0	3.1	3.7	4.9
1c	0.6	1.0	2.1	9.3	11.2	14.8
2	0.9	1.3	2.9	0.7	0.8	1.1
3	33.1	0.0	0.0	17.2	0.0	0.0
4	3.8	5.7	5.6	2.5	3.0	3.0
4a	0.9	1.4	3.0	0.5	0.6	0.8
4b	0.3	0.5	1.1	0.6	0.7	0.9
5	1.8	2.8	3.9	1.2	1.4	1.3
6	12.6	20.0	0.0	6.5	8.2	0.0
7	6.3	9.5	12.8	8.2	9.8	8.1
8	0.9	1.3	2.8	0.9	1.1	1.4
8a	0.4	0.5	1.2	0.2	0.2	0.3
8b	0.0	0.1	0.1	0.0	0.1	0.1
8c	0.1	0.1	0.3	0.2	0.3	0.4
9	0.8	1.3	0.0	0.7	0.8	0.0
9a	0.4	0.7	0.0	0.2	0.2	0.0
9b	0.0	0.0	0.0	0.0	0.0	0.0
9c	0.1	0.2	0.0	0.3	0.4	0.0
10	0.8	1.2	0.0	0.3	0.4	0.0
11	7.0	10.5	9.8	4.4	5.3	3.8
12	13.6	19.2	3.5	7.7	8.9	1.8
Total	100.0	100.0	100.0	100.0	100.0	100.0

Note: Based on four observations during a year and a half for each individual during 1995–2003.
Source: Calculations based on EPH—INDEC.

identify the differences in the hazard rates for all destinations, and competing risks are assessed.[37]

Exit rates diminish monotonically with time in state, indicating negative duration dependence.[38] Job-specific human capital plays a role: the employer who pays to train

37. Specifically, two different regressions were performed for all workers from a simple specification (regression I), to which the nonproportional effect of being young on the baseline hazard was then added (regression II). Separate regressions were also performed for young workers (regression III) and adult workers (regression IV), for each occupational category (regressions V, VI, and VII), and for men (regression VIII) and women (regression IX).

38. Similar results are reported in Beccaria and Maurizio (2003) and in Galiani and Hopenhayn (2000).

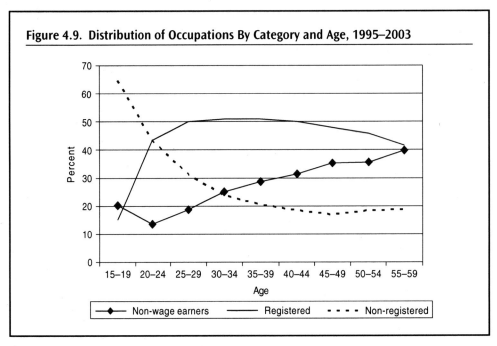

Figure 4.9. Distribution of Occupations By Category and Age, 1995–2003

Source: Calculations based on EPH.

employees is interested in retaining them.[39] As duration in a job rises, so does the probability that individuals have more stable paths and so lower exit rates from the job. Labor regulations are also important: most regulations tie firing costs to the time spent on the job, an additional disincentive to dismiss skilled, experienced workers.

Occupational exit rate differences between young and adult groups vary across tenure duration. Adult workers achieve job stability more quickly than youth, even controlling for other variables.[40]

A youth's chance of leaving a job exceeds that of an adult by 17–30 percent, reflecting both supply and demand factors. Alternative activities (studying, for example) encourage higher rotation (supply). Partly as a result, youth are considered less reliable by employers and so are placed in more unstable positions (demand). Lastly, young workers—because of their age—generally have less work experience and shorter job tenure, making them more likely targets for dismissal.

An inverse correlation exists between age and the chances of working in nonregistered jobs (Figure 4.9). So some of the high turnover of young workers may be due to their

39. Another explanation for the relationship between job duration and the probability of exit focuses on the quality of the matching between the requirements of a job and the capacities of the worker. Neither is known beforehand. If the quality of matching is inadequate, it will probably lead to the termination of the agreement. Because matching information is usually obtained during the first months of the contract, this theory provides an additional explanation for the higher rotation during the first months on the job. A third explanation examines the heterogeneity of the labor force and argues that the probability of finding workers with higher instability in the shorter duration strata is higher because they have small chances of reaching long durations.

40. In the interval from three to five years, however, the difference is smaller than for the previous interval, though still positive.

concentration in precarious jobs. Youth, however, have 27 percent higher rotation rates even in the formal sector, suggesting that younger workers have higher occupational instability for other reasons as well. Youth may have less job tenure and fewer specific skills than adults, making it cheaper for employers to dismiss them.[41]

Several factors explain why registered workers have more stability than unregistered workers. With low legal firing costs, unregistered workers appeal to employers in industries with unstable demand. An employer may also decide not to register an employee to test the worker for longer than the official trial period—or as an alternative to it. Moreover, employees not covered by social security are more prevalent in small and informal firms. Because they operate with low capital-labor ratios, the decision to interrupt economic activity—and layoff workers—is easier. In contrast, registered wage earners have higher firing costs and receive more job-specific training.

Schooling is inversely correlated with the probability of leaving a job, with the highest instability among the least educated workers. Education is associated with needed job skills, and general and specific human capital are usually complementary. So the most educated workers receive more specific training, encouraging employers to retain them—incentives that grow as workers spend more time on the job. The most educated workers also more frequently work in registered jobs.

Men and household heads have less instability than women and those not heads of households, though the gaps are smaller than those between occupation categories. Women's higher instability is usually explained by family responsibilities and cultural patterns— cultural patterns that may be reinforced by employers who see higher rotation among women and then discriminate against them. Employers may place women in unstable jobs, even if they have the same education as men—as with youth. Differences among age groups are larger for men than women, suggesting that the instability differences between youth and adult workers are greater for more stable groups (registered wage earners and men).

Several other factors affect instability. Construction has a higher exit rate than manufacturing, while public sector jobs are the most stable. Geographically, greater Buenos Aires is the most stable urban area for youth but the least stable for adults.

Young women with low education and unregistered wage earners face the highest labor turnover—a result particularly important because of the high proportion of youth working in precarious, unregistered jobs.

Competing Risks

This section examines separately exits to another job, unemployment, and out of the labor force. First, negative duration dependence is strongly verified in all three cases, especially in exits to another job and to unemployment. For exits from the labor force or to unemployment a lower hazard rate is observed at higher durations, although no differences exist between youth and adult groups.

Youth have high rates of transition to unemployment and out of the labor force, but not to another job, suggesting that the higher youth exit rates in the previous section are due mainly to more transitions from a job to nonemployment (unemployment or out of

---

41. Segregation may be underestimated, however, since the high exit rates of registered young workers may indicate that they are more often in more unstable, though registered, jobs.

the workforce). Competing risk analysis shows that youth have a 25 percent higher probability of exiting to unemployment than adults and a 29 percent higher probability of leaving the labor force. The similarities in rates of exit to another job may reflect a lower chance that young workers will find another job after leaving their current one. So the young face both higher occupation instability and more transitions to unemployment and inactivity.

As in the previous discussion, competing risk analysis shows that the probability of exiting to another job, unemployment, or inactivity decreases with education. Workers with university education have fewer job exits and, when they leave, more transitions to another job (compared with unemployment or inactivity). Men and household heads also have a lower probability than women or those not heads of households of exiting the labor force and a higher probability of going to another job or unemployment.[42]

The Challenges of Unemployment, Instability, and Early Labor Force Entry

"I'm working right now, but I'm always wondering if I might get fired, and I'm looking for another job just in case because I know there's no sustainability"

—Agustín, 25 years old, Cordoba

Although young people are more educated today, some face difficult job prospects. Youth face hazard rates more than 17 percent higher than those of adults, and higher youth unemployment leaves three young people unemployed for every adult unemployed.

Youth who found jobs tended to work in the informal sectors, earning less money with less job security. Working hours fell sharply for youth since the early 1990s. Education helps, leading to higher wage returns, especially for tertiary-educated youth. Higher education also protected youth against unemployment during economic downturns. Young people, however, have far lower returns than adults to all levels of education, even controlling for experience and other factors. The least educated young workers face the highest job instability.

Youth fared badly during business cycles. Suffering more in recessions, youth also recovered more slowly during expansions. Business cycles hit primary-school graduates the hardest.

Some questions that may guide policy discussions on youth labor issues include:

- How is the economy best stabilized and growth ensured in order not to hurt youth employment and wages?
- What is the most effective strategy to tackle instability, informality, and unemployment among young workers, especially the young women who are most affected?
- How can an excessively early entry into the labor force that cuts short education and damages future prospects be best avoided?
- What is the most effective strategy to address inactivity or idleness among youth, which can potentially lead to risky behaviors?
- How can the effects of unemployment, which hits the most vulnerable—youth from poor households—especially hard, be best mitigated?

---

42. Similar results are reported in Beccaria and Maurizio (2003).

CHAPTER 5

Growing Up Healthy

By Georgina Binstock and Alessandra Heinemann

"We go right from the pediatrician to the clinic."

—Anonymous young Argentine

Good health is important to well-being and future productivity. However, young people can be prone to risky behavior that severely undermines their future health. Risky behaviors such as smoking, alcohol abuse, and drug use not only exacerbate the public health burden, but also produce negative outcomes for the individual, such as poor educational attainment, reduced productivity, increased absenteeism, traffic accidents, and violence.[43] Health-related risky behaviors are often associated with each other: excessive drinking negatively impacts academic performance and increases the risk of being a victim of crime (see Table 1.2 in Chapter 1 for the framework of associated risky behaviors) (DeSimore and Delaware 2005). At the same time, excessive alcohol consumption is correlated with unprotected sex, which increases the risk of contracting sexually-transmitted diseases (STDs) or getting pregnant (see Chapter 6 for a discussion of reproductive health) (Markovitz, Kaestner, and Grossman 2006).

Overall, youth in Argentina are healthier today than at any time in history, but youth mortality—at 50 deaths per 100,000 females and 120 per 100,000 males—is higher than expected for a country of its income (Table 5.1). The National Risk Factor Survey found that 39.8 percent of youth in Argentina have low levels of physical activity, 17.9 percent are overweight, and 3.9 percent obese (Ministerio de Salud 2006). Mental health issues are also

---

43. Haggerty and others (1996); Garmezy and Rutter (1983); for ecological approaches: Bronfenbrenner (1979, 1986); social capital approaches: Coleman (1988); and resource approaches: Brooks-Gunn and others (1993), Haveman and Wolfe (1994).

Table 5.1. Mortality Rate for Ages 15–24 (per 100,000 inhabitants; most recent year available)

Country	Youth Aged 15–24		
	Total	Female	Male
Argentina (2005)	80	50	120
Brazil (1998)	153	76	230
Chile (1999)	74	36	111
Costa Rica (2001)	66	34	97
Mexico (2000)	101	53	149
Spain (2000)	49	25	73
Uruguay (2004)	130	71	186

Source: Argentina: National Institute for Statistics and Census (2005); Brazil, Costa Rica, Mexico, and Spain: CEPAL (2004); Chile: National Census (2003); Uruguay: National Census (2004).

Table 5.2. Mortality Due to External Causes, Ages 15–24 (2005)

	Male	Female
Accidents	1641	434
Suicides	639	148
Aggressions	529	60

Ministerio de Salud (2007).

Table 5.3. Projected Numbers of 15-year-Olds in 2003 Who Will Die Before the Age of 60 (per 1,000)

Country	Female	Male
Argentina	90	176
Brazil	129	240
Chile	66	133
Costa Rica	79	129
Italy	47	93
Mexico	95	166
Spain	46	116
Uruguay	87	180
Venezuela	97	181

Source: World Bank (2006b).

a concern, as 14.9 percent of youth experience moderate anxiety or depression and suicides make up 14.6 percent of deaths for 15–24-year-olds (see Table 5.2; Ministerio de Salud 2007). While these figures provide some indication of the state of health of the youth population, they do not adequately reflect whether youth are taking risks that may jeopardize their health in the future. More appropriate benchmarks include behaviors that put health at risk later in life, including tobacco and drug use and excessive alcohol consumption. For instance, smoking is estimated to cause more than 40,000 deaths and the loss of 824,804 healthy life years in Argentina (MSN 2005). Alcohol consumption is estimated to cause the loss of 331,802 disability-adjusted life years (DALYs; Ministerio de Salud 2006). The probability that a 15-year-old girl in Argentina will die before the age of 60 is almost twice as high as in Spain, and for boys it is more than 50 percent higher (Table 5.3).

Nearly two-thirds of premature deaths and one-third of the total disease burden of adults can be associated with conditions or behaviors begun in youth. The impact of risk-taking behavior on health care expenditures and GDP is also considerable. For instance, individual country studies estimate that the net cost of tobacco use is between 0.03 and 0.4 percent of GDP (World Bank 1999). A study by the Ministry of Health of schools in the five most populous cities in Argentina shows that 60 percent of adolescents have tried tobacco and 20 percent smoke habitually. More alarming, the age at which youth start smoking is going down (Ministerio de Salud 2003). While health coverage is key to effectively implementing prevention and control strategies, only 54.8 percent of youth have health coverage. The proportion of the total population with health coverage is significantly higher at 65.1 percent (Ministerio de Salud 2006).

Traffic injury is one of the leading causes of death among youth, especially for young males—in 2005, 665 youth died in traffic accidents.[44] The mortality rate per 100,000 due to traffic injuries is 15.03 for males and 4.07 for females (Table 5.4). These figures

Table 5.4. Mortality per 100,000 Caused by Road Traffic Injury for Ages 15–29 (most recent year available)

Country	Males	Females
Argentina (2005)	15.0	4.1
Brazil (1995)	44.3	11.1
Chile (1999)	15.0	3.8
Uruguay (2000)	18.2	n/a

Source: Argentina: Ministry of Health, Statistics, and Health Information (2005); Brazil, Chile, and Uruguay: WHO (2004a).

are lower than the LAC regional average of 31.2 per 100,000 for males and 8.7 per 100,000 for females ages 15–29, however (WHO 2004b). Homicide is another significant cause of death for young males, although rates are far lower than the regional average.[45] Among young females one of the leading avoidable causes of death is complications resulting from abortion, which is illegal in Argentina and therefore often conducted in unsanitary conditions. Up to 50 percent of maternal deaths can be attributed to complications from abortion (see Chapter 6).[46]

In Argentina there is little suitable data on the effects of youth health and health behaviors on health outcomes during adulthood.[47] This chapter seeks to contribute to the knowledge of youth health behavior by describing patterns of risk-taking and identifying factors associated with these behaviors. Recognizing these patterns and factors associated with risk is a prerequisite for designing effective preventive health strategies. In particular, the chapter focuses on young people's use of addictive substances, including tobacco, alcohol, and drugs. The final section raises some questions for health policy.

Tobacco—Youth Are Starting to Smoke Younger

Many youth in Argentina smoke, and they are starting at younger and younger ages (Ministerio de Salud 2006). Compared with Venezuela, the percentage of 13–15-year-old Argentines who smoke is almost three times as high for girls and more than twice as high for boys (Table 5.5). More than 37 percent of youth ages 15–24 reported having smoked in the past in the YSCS, and about half of them smoke on a regular basis (18.3 percent; Table 5.6). The proportion of regular smokers is higher among men (20.9 percent) than among

---

44. See www.deis.gov.ar/publicaciones/archivos/Serie5Nro49.pdf, Table 24.

45. The WHO estimates homicide rates per 100,000 people for males ages 15–29 at 11.5 in Argentina and the corresponding homicide rate for females at 2.0 (WHO 2002). See Chapter 7 for a more detailed discussion of violence and proxy homicide rates based on indictment rates for more recent years.

46. The data on the proportion of maternal deaths due to complications from abortion vary from 27 percent (CEDES 2004) to 50 percent when correcting for underreporting (Ministry of Health).

47. Most of the studies in this area refer to the age, gender, educational, and socioeconomic profile of tobacco, alcohol, and drug users. Míguez (1998, 2000).

Table 5.5. Tobacco Use in Adolescents

Country	Year	Percentage of People Ages 13–15	
		Female	Male
Argentina	2000	34	31
Brazil	2002	18	21
Chile	2000	42	33
Costa Rica	2002	19	20
Mexico	2002	20	24
Uruguay	2001	26	22
Venezuela	2003	12	15

Source: World Bank (2006b).

women (15.8 percent).[48] The average starting age for those now ages 18–24 is 15.8 years for females and 16.6 for males, down from 17.1 and 17.5 respectively for the age group now 25–35. The lower starting age has been especially marked for young women.

Public policy interest arises out of the concern that young people in Argentina do not appropriately recognize the long-run consequences of their smoking habits and the impact on public health. Studies of adolescents in the United States and Colombia have also identified tobacco as a gateway to marijuana and other drugs. So, identifying risk factors associated with smoking is necessary for effectively targeting youth with smoking prevention campaigns.

Smoking is most common among youth who work, youth who are not attending school, and youth who consume alcohol (Table 5.6). Thirty-three percent of youth who work smoke, compared with 12.9 percent of those who do not work—perhaps because smoking is not banned in all workplaces and because youth have more money to buy tobacco, which has high demand elasticity. Dropping out of school is also associated with smoking regularly among the youngest males: 40 percent of men aged 15–19 who are not attending high school smoke regularly. There is also a strong association between smoking and drinking: 25 percent of youth who drink are regular smokers, while only 6.6 percent of those who do not drink are smokers (Míguez and Pecci 1994).

Young men are 40 percent more likely to smoke than young women, controlling for all other variables. Living with both parents decreases young people's probability of smoking regularly, compared with living with only one parent (Table 5.7). Socioeconomic background and the mother's level of education do not have a significant effect on the probability of smoking. City of residence also has no measurable effect. Attending school and not working appear as protective factors against smoking regularly—odds are about 90 percent higher for those who do not attend school than for those who do and about 50 percent higher for those who work than for those who do not. The association between alcohol consumption and smoking is significant, even when controlling for other factors. Those who drink are 234 percent more likely to smoke than young people who do not.

Alcohol Consumption Is Highly Associated with Other Risky Behaviors

Excessive alcohol consumption not only undermines people's health but is also a key contributing factor to traffic accidents, violence, and risky sexual behavior. The WHO estimates that alcohol consumption causes 3.2 percent of deaths (1.8 million) worldwide

48. The National Risk Factor Survey estimates the proportion of youth smokers ages 18–24 at 36.1 percent (Ministerio de Salud 2006).

Table 5.6. Patterns of Tobacco Use for Youth Ages 15–24

Selected Characteristics	Tobacco Use			
	Regular	Sporadic	Past	Never
Total	18.3	10.6	8.3	62.8
Age: 15 to 19	13.0	9.9	7.7	69.4
Age : 20 to 24	27.2	11.6	9.3	51.9
Male	20.9	10.6	7.6	60.9
Female	15.8	10.5	9.1	64.6
School attendance: Yes	11.8	8.7	9.2	70.3
School attendance: No	30.1	14.0	6.8	49.1
Labor participation: Work	33.9	14.6	7.0	44.5
Labor participation: Does not work	12.9	9.2	8.8	69.1
Socioeconomic status*: High	37.8	22.4	11.3	28.5
Socioeconomic status*: Middle	15.9	13.9	12.4	57.8
Socioeconomic status*: Low	17.9	9.0	7.0	66.1
Mother's education				
Up to high school incomplete	20.7	10.9	7.6	60.8
Completed high school or more	15.1	10.1	9.4	65.4
Lives with: Both parents	15.1	7.4	7.3	70.2
Lives with: Only with mother	18.2	17.8	9.9	54.1
Lives with: Others	30.3	11.5	9.7	48.5
Drinks alcohol: Yes	25.0	14.2	10.5	50.3
Drinks alcohol: No	6.6	4.3	4.6	84.5
Plays sports: Yes	15.4	10.0	8.3	66.3
Plays sports: No	21.1	11.1	8.3	59.5
Parent smokes regularly**: Yes	24.0	15.4	4.8	55.8
Parent smokes regularly**: No	11.8	7.0	4.2	77.0
Greater Buenos Aires	18.4	10.1	8.2	63.3
Salta	14.7	21.1	11.0	53.2
Neuquén	16.2	18.8	8.9	56.1
Posadas	16.9	12.7	8.9	61.5

Note:
*Socioeconomic background indicator employed by FLACSO.
**Includes only youth with information on parents (48.2 percent of the sample).
Source: Calculations based on YSCS.

and more than 60 types of disease and injury (WHO 2004a). Long-term excessive alcohol consumption can result in liver disease, cancer, cardiovascular disease, and neurological damage and psychiatric problems (CDC 2006). Alcohol use reduces self-control and the ability to process incoming information, and it can increase emotional liability

Table 5.7. Estimated Relative Odds of Smoking Frequently

Independent Variables	Odds Ratio
Intercept	−1.82[a]
Age	
15 to 19	1.05
20 to 24	
Gender	
Male	1.40[c]
Female	
Mother's education	
Up to high school incomplete	0.95
Completed high school or more	
Lives with	
Both parents	0.66[b]
Only with mother	1.07
Others	
Socioeconomic status	
High	1.44
Middle	
Low	0.77
City	
Salta	0.81
Neuquén	1.06
Posadas	0.71
Greater Buenos Aires	
School attendance	
Yes	0.54[a]
No	
Labor participation	
Work	1.44[b]
Does not work	
Alcohol consumption	
Drinks	3.34[a]
Does not drink	
Plays sports	
Yes	0.79
No	

[a]p < .001; [b]p < .05; [c]p < .10.

Note: These are odds ratios estimated with a binomial logistic regression model. Odds ratios will also be employed in the remaining sections of this chapter. If the odds ratios are reduced by 1 and then multiplied by 100, they indicate the percentage increase (if greater than 1) or decrease (if less than 1) in the odds of smoking frequently associated with each unit increase of the explanatory variable.

Source: Calculations based on YSCS.

and impulsiveness. In Argentina 37 percent of traffic accidents among males and 47 percent of homicides and aggressions can be attributed to alcohol consumption (see Chapter 7; Ministerio de Salud 2006). Individual and societal beliefs about the effects of alcohol often mean that people drink to prepare for violence (Ohene, Ireland, and Blum 2005). Alcohol use is also a risk factor for intimate partner violence and risky sexual behavior.

Argentines, especially young males, are consuming alcohol earlier in life and in a more risky and harmful manner than earlier generations. Among those ages 15–24, 9.4 percent drink alcohol frequently and 54.1 percent drink sporadically (Table 5.8). Both frequent and sporadic alcohol consumption are more common among young men than among young women (58.7 and 49.7 percent compared with 12.6 and 6.3 percent, respectively). Alcohol abuse is highest in the 16–24 age group (11 percent; Míguez 2000). Of males ages 18–24, 18.5 percent binge drink on weekends, although only 2.5 percent of females do (Ministerio de Salud 2006). This rising alcohol consumption among youth is a result of cultural change that promotes binge drinking (Míguez 2000).

The pattern of alcohol consumption in Argentina reveals four characteristics common in youth who drink frequently: being male, not attending school, working, and smoking (Table 5.8). As in the case of tobacco consumption, young people who attend school are less prone to drink frequently than those who do not, although there are no differences in the sporadic use of

Table 5.8. Patterns of Alcohol Use for Youth Ages 15–24

	Alcohol Drinking			
	Frequent	Sporadic	Past	Never
Total	9.4	54.1	1.4	35.2
Age				
15 to 19	9.1	52.8	1.3	36.7
20 to 24	9.8	56.2	1.5	32.5
Gender				
Male	12.6	58.7	0.4	28.4
Female	6.3	49.7	2.3	41.7
School attendance				
Yes	7.3	55.2	0.9	36.6
No	13.1	52.1	2.2	32.6
Labor participation				
Work	15	55.6	2.8	26.6
Does not work	7.5	53.6	0.9	38.1
Socioeconomic status				
High	0.8	80.5	0.6	18
Middle	5.8	66.8	0.8	26.6
Low	10.9	49	1.6	38.6
Mother's education				
Up to high school incomplete	7.9	50.6	1.9	39.6
Completed high school or more	11.4	58.8	0.6	29.2
Lives with				
Both parents	9.7	55.4	1	33.9
Mother only	9.8	53.3	2.8	34.1
Others	7.5	50.2	0.6	41.8
Smokes tobacco				
No	6.6	51.6	1.6	40.2
Yes	21.7	65.1	0.3	12.9
Plays sports				
Yes	7.4	54.4	0.7	37.5
No	11.3	53.8	2	32.8
City				
Greater Buenos Aires	9.8	54.4	1	34.8
Salta	1.4	50	6	42.6
Neuquén	2.8	42.8	8.5	45.9
Posadas	5.8	56.8	3.5	33.9

Source: Calculations based on YSCS.

alcohol between the two groups. Employed youth have a higher incidence of regular drinking than those who are not employed—but working does not affect sporadic use of alcohol.[49]

When looking at relative odds, gender and city of residence are associated with the probability of drinking alcohol (Table 5.9). Men are twice as likely to drink regularly as women. City differences are pronounced: young people in greater Buenos Aires have the highest probability of drinking alcohol, while the probability is lowest in Salta, suggesting that social tolerance or availability of alcohol in each city may differ. Young people who smoke regularly are three times more likely to drink regularly than those who do not smoke or smoke sporadically.

Illegal Drug Use Is Fairly Low, but Usually Starts during Youth

The use of illegal drugs is relatively low in Argentina, but first drug use usually occurs early in life.[50] Among YSCS respondents 2 percent reported currently using drugs, but 10 percent declared having consumed drugs in the past (Table 5.10). Most current users consume drugs sporadically (45 percent), 10 percent on a monthly basis, 26 percent on a weekly basis, and 19 percent on a daily basis. While 18.6 percent of men reported having current or past experience with drugs, only 7.1 percent of women did. Marijuana is the preferred drug among youth—almost 90 percent of current drug users report using it.

With the exception of socioeconomic background, all considered variables—age, gender, mother's education, residence with parents, and city of residence—are significantly associated with the probability of having used drugs (Table 5.11). Male youth are 160 percent more likely to have experimented with drugs than female youth. Living with both parents is a strong protective factor, as is attending school.

Young people who smoke regularly and youth who drink alcohol are more than twice as likely to have used drugs as their peers. Although the nature of these links cannot be established conclusively, they suggest that preventive programs for smoking and alcohol abuse may also help prevent drug use. Playing sports, which was not a significant factor in explaining regular smoking or drinking, is a significant protective factor against drug use—youth who play a sport are about half as likely to have consumed drugs.

City of residence is also highly associated with drug use—youth in greater Buenos Aires are the most likely to have used drugs. This independent effect of city of residence could be due to social control, local differences in social acceptance of risky behaviors, the availability of substances, or the structure of opportunities for youth in each city. Youth

---

49. This result may be indicative of the use of alcohol at work. If this is the case (something that cannot be answered on the basis of the YSCS data), it may constitute part of a larger problem regarding the use of psychoactive substances to cope with tension or frustration at work (Míguez 1998).

50. The 2006 World Drug Report, which provides an overall assessment on the incidence of illegal drug use all over the world, found that 2.9 percent of Argentines reported having used illegal drugs in the last 30 days, which is below the world average of 4.9 percent for those ages 15–64.

employment also stands out as a risk factor for drug use. Further research with appropriate longitudinal data (or retrospective life history data) will be needed to shed light on the effect labor force participation has on risk-taking behavior. The fact that socioeconomic background does not appear to be a significant predictor of drug use may suggest that some youth lifestyle habits are converging across socioeconomic backgrounds. However, quality and quantity of the substances used may differ across income groups.

Promoting Healthy Lives

"It won't happen to me."

—Anonymous young Argentine

Young Argentines are a healthy group overall, but a substantial proportion of them engage in risky behavior that will affect their well-being and productive capacity long into the future, as well as drive up the public health burden. Young males are most likely to jeopardize their future health by smoking, abusing alcohol, and consuming drugs. As the analysis in the previous sections illustrates, these risk factors are closely correlated with each other, with smoking increasing the likelihood of drinking and vice versa. On the other hand, attending school and living with both parents consistently appear as protective factors.

Some of the risks young people take can be easily prevented—and at low cost. But even when young people have information about the danger of certain behaviors, they continue to make poor choices.

Table 5.9. Estimated Relative Odds of Drinking Alcohol on a Regular Basis

Independent Variables	Odds Ratio
Intercept	-3.36[a]
Age	
15 to 19	0.81
20 to 24	
Gender	
Male	2.02[b]
Female	
Mother's education	
Up to high school incomplete	0.65
Completed high school or more	
Lives with	
Both parents	1.46
Mother only	1.08
Others	
Socioeconomic status	
High	0.84
Middle	
Low	1.3
City	
Salta	0.24[a]
Neuquén	0.38[b]
Posadas	0.96
Greater Buenos Aires	
School attendance	
Yes	0.85
No	
Labor participation	
Work	1.85[b]
Does not work	
Smokes frequently	
Yes	4.02[a]
No	
Plays sports	
Yes	0.62
No	

[a]$p < .001$; [b]$p < .05$; [c]$p < .10$.
Source: Calculations based on YSCS.

Table 5.10. Patterns of Drug Use for Youth Ages 15–24

	Drug Use		
	Current	**Past**	**Never**
Total	2.0	10.0	88.0
Age			
15 to 19	0.5	6.5	93.0
20 to 24	4.5	15.9	79.6
Gender			
Male	3.6	15.0	81.4
Female	0.4	5.3	94.3
School attendance			
Yes	0.8	6.3	92.9
No	4.0	16.7	79.3
Labor participation			
Work	2.5	19.5	78.0
Does not work	1.8	6.8	91.5
Socioeconomic status			
High	10.3	16.7	73.0
Middle	5.0	12.8	82.2
Low	0.6	8.9	90.5
Mother's education			
Up to high school incomplete	2.0	10.5	87.5
Completed high school or more	1.9	9.4	88.7
Lives with			
Both parents	0.6	9.5	89.9
Mother only	3.5	7.0	89.6
Others	5.0	16.7	78.3
Smokes tobacco regularly			
No	0.9	5.1	94.0
Yes	6.6	32.3	61.1
Drinks alcohol			
Yes	3.1	14.3	82.6
No	0.0	2.5	97.5
Plays sports			
Yes	1.9	9.1	89.0
No	2.0	10.9	87.1
City			
Greater Buenos Aires	2.0	10.3	87.7
Salta	1.2	5.9	92.9
Neuquén	1.8	6.3	91.9
Posadas	1.4	5.0	93.5

Source: Calculations based on YSCS.

Recently, public health interventions have focused on teaching at-risk groups life skills, including the ability to think critically, to be assertive, and to understand the influence of community, family, and gender in decisionmaking. It is important to evaluate public health interventions carefully, focusing on changes in young people's behavior, rather than just increased knowledge.

Because health habits are formed during youth, it is important to invest in young people's health and minimize their risk-taking. In order to avoid future health care expenditures and the loss of human capital, polices could aim to (1) give young people the capacity to make informed choices about their behavior and the skills to negotiate safe behavior with peers and partners; (2) create an environment that is conducive to healthy behavior, limiting the scope for risk-taking; and (3) offer second chances though treatment and rehabilitation for those harmed by poor health decisions (World Bank 2006b).

Some questions that may guide policy discussions regarding health challenges are:

- Because school attendance appears to play an important role in restraining youth from smoking regularly or from experimenting with drugs, how can youth best be helped to continue building their skills and encouraged to stay in school?
- Which preventive programs for smoking and alcohol abuse are best suited to the Argentine context?

Table 5.11. Estimated Relative Odds of Having Consumed Drugs

Independent Variables	Odds Ratio
Intercept	−2.50[a]
Age	
15 to 19	0.73
20 to 24	
Gender	
Male	2.63[a]
Female	
Mother's education	
Up to high school incomplete	1.34
Completed high school or more	
Lives with	
Both parents	0.69
Mother only	0.76
Others	
Socioeconomic status	
High	0.88
Middle	
Low	0.68
City	
Salta	0.51[a]
Neuquén	0.52[a]
Posadas	0.29[a]
Greater Buenos Aires	
School attendance	
Yes	0.48
No	
Labor participation	
Work	1.38
Does not work	
Smokes frequently	
Yes	3.44[a]
No	
Drinks alcohol	
Yes	3.49[a]
No	
Plays sports	
Yes	0.55[b]
No	

[a] $p < .001$; [b] $p < .05$; [c] $p < .10$.

Note: Odds ratios estimated using a binomial logistic regression model. If the odds ratios are reduced by 1 and then multiplied by 100, they indicate the percentage increase (if greater than 1) or decrease (if less than 1) in the rates drug use associated with each unit of the explanatory variable.

Source: Calculations based on YSCS.

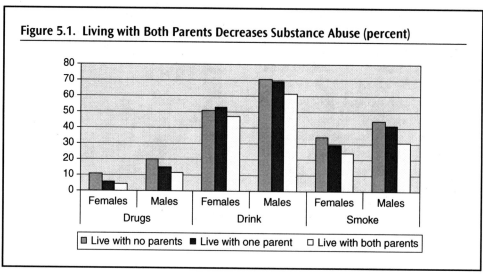

Figure 5.1. Living with Both Parents Decreases Substance Abuse (percent)

Source: Calculations on YSCS.

- Is increasing the price of cigarettes and alcohol a potentially effective tool to reduce youth consumption?
- Can minimum age purchase laws reduce the incidence of binge drinking?
- Does advertising encourage substance abuse and can a ban reduce the incidence of smoking and drinking?

CHAPTER 6

Forming Families

By Georgina Binstock and Alessandra Heinemann

"The concept of family has broken down."

—Emiliano, 17-year-old high school student, city of Buenos Aires

Although sexual initiation is no longer necessarily connected to marriage and childbearing, it continues to be an important factor in the transition to adulthood.[51] Biological, psychological, family, peer, and socio-cultural factors all influence sexual behavior.[52] The family's reproductive history—especially the mother's—strongly influences young people's reproductive decisions. Furthermore, the higher the level of education achieved by the parents, the higher the educational and professional goals they set for their children, which reduces fertility and dependency. Youth who stay in school tend to be more goal-orientated and have higher educational and professional expectations, which may prevent them from engaging in risky behavior. Recent research finds that working is conducive to sexual initiation, which supports the hypothesis that making an early transition into an adult role by working may speed the onset of other adult behaviors (Bozick 2006). At the same time, working appears to increase the opportunity cost of an early pregnancy and thus leads to a higher use of contraception.

The economic and social costs of early pregnancies are huge—for young mothers, for young fathers, and for their children. A threat to the health of mother and child, early pregnancy can diminish both parents' productivity, earnings, and human capital. Children

---

51. Udry and Campbell (1994). Due to the lack of representative national data sources, most quantitative research on sexual initiation has been based on restricted samples, focusing on youth who are in school or use public health services (Gogna 2005).

52. See Miller and Moore (1990) for a review.

Table 6.1. Economic and Social Costs of Early Pregnancies

Adolescent mothers	▦ Higher probability of raising their children in poverty
	▦ Lower education
	▦ Lower earnings, productivity, and savings
	▦ Higher welfare dependency
Adolescent fathers	▦ Lower education
	▦ Lower earnings, productivity, and savings
	▦ Not a consistent support for adolescent mothers and their children
Children	▦ Lower quality home environment
	▦ Reduced cognitive development and educational attainment
	▦ Greater likelihood of delayed entry in school or grade repetition during adolescence
	▦ Lower healthcare use, health spending, and health insurance, leading to worse health outcomes
	▦ Higher rates of abuse and neglect leading to placement in foster homes or orphanages
	▦ Increased risk of behavior problems, incarceration, and substance abuse

Source: World Bank (forthcoming).

born to young parents are more likely to struggle with cognitive development and educational attainment (Table 6.1).

Adequately preparing young people for parenthood helps society by decreasing fertility and dependency. It opens a window of opportunity for human capital accumulation, productivity gains, economic growth, and poverty reduction. Adequate preparation for family formation can thus ensure that well-being, rather than poverty, is transmitted to the next generation.

One in six Argentine mothers gives birth between ages 15 and 19, and adolescent fertility is even higher in some provinces. At 61 births per 1,000 people, the fertility rate for girls 15–19 is below the Latin American average of 72 but higher than in neighboring Chile (44 births per 1,000 people) (UNICEF 2006). For instance, the rate in Chaco is over 100 births per 1,000 people, which is comparable to rates for Africa (Binstock and Pantelides 2005). The percentage of repeat pregnancies among women below the age of 20 was 22 percent overall and 29.3 percent in Chaco in 2005 (Ministerio de Salud 2007).

Table 6.2. Child Mortality Indicators, Selected Countries (per 1,000 births)

	Under-5 Mortality (2005)	Infant Mortality (Under 1) (2005)
Argentina	15.5	13.3
Brazil	120	87
Chile	10	8
France	5	4
Mexico	27	22
Uruguay	15	14

Source: UNICEF (2006) and Ministerio de Salud (2005).

Table 6.3. Child Heath Indicators, Selected Countries

	Percentage of Infants With Low Birth Weight (under 2,500 grams), 1998–2005*	Percentage of Children Under Five Suffering from Moderate and Severe Ailments 1996–2005:*		
		Underweight[+]	Wasting[++]	Stunting[+++]
Argentina	8	4	1	4
Brazil	8	6	2	11
Chile	6	1	0	1
Italy	6	N/A	N/A	N/A
Mexico	8	8	2	18
Uruguay	8	5**	1**	8**

*Data refer to the most recent year available.
**Data refer to years or periods other than those specified in the column heading, differ from the standard definition, or refer to only part of a country.
[+]Two standard deviations below median weight for age.
[++]Two standard deviations below median weight for height.
[+++]Two standard deviations below median height for age.
Source: UNICEF (2006).

More Argentine children are born with low birth weight—more common for young mothers—than expected for a country with its GDP (Table 6.3). With 8 percent of its infants born underweight, Argentina is close to the regional average of 9 percent.[53] About 4 percent of children under five suffer from moderate or severe stunting, with a similar share moderately or severely underweight. While Argentina does better than the regional averages of 15 percent stunted and 7 percent underweight, it does worse than Chile, where only 1 percent of children under five are stunted or underweight.[54] Furthermore, child mortality is significantly higher in Argentina than in Chile—15.5 children die under age 5 for every 1,000 born, compared with just 10 deaths in Chile (Table 6.2). Yet, infant mortality rates have fallen recently, showing that health policies can make a difference.

With abortion illegal and often conducted secretly in unsafe conditions, complications from abortion is one of the leading preventable causes of death for young women. Maternal mortality is also surprisingly high—more than double that in Chile and Uruguay—despite widespread antenatal care and the nearly universal presence of skilled attendants at delivery (Table 6.4). However, adolescent mortality (ages 10–19) as a share of total of maternal deaths has decreased significantly from 14 percent in 1999 to 9.3 percent in 2005 (Ministerio de Salud 2007). Of these deaths, 30.8 percent were due to complications with abortion.[55]

---

53. Low birth weight is defined as infants weighing less than 2,500 grams. Data for the most recent year available 1998–2005 (UNICEF 2006).

54. Ibid.

55. According to official figures, abortion complications cause approximately 27 percent of maternal deaths (CEDES 2004), but the Ministry of Health estimates that, correcting for underreporting, abortions cause about half of maternal deaths. Health complications due to clandestine abortion is one of the main causes of maternal death in the country (Ramos and others 2004).

Table 6.4. Maternal Health Indicators, Selected Countries

	Antenatal Care Coverage (percent) 1997–2005*	Skilled Attendant at Delivery (percent) 1997–2005*	Maternal Mortality Ratio[+]		
			1990–2005* Reported	Adjusted (2000)	Lifetime Risk of Maternal Death. (2000) 1 in:
Argentina	98	99	40	82	410
Brazil	97	97	72	260	140
Chile	95**	100	17	31	1100
France	99**	99**	10	17	2700
Mexico	86**	83	63	83	370
Uruguay	94	100	26	27	1300

[+]Data in the column "reported" are those reported by national authorities. Periodically, UNICEF, WHO, and UUNFPA adjust the data to account for underreporting and misclassification of maternal deaths. Adjusted estimates reflect the most recent reviews (2000).
*Data refer to the most recent year available.
**Data refer to years or periods other than those specified in the column heading, differ from the standard definition, or refer to only part of a country.
Source: UNICEF (2006).

Health and family policies must prepare youth for the transition to parenthood, ensuring planned childbearing, safe pregnancy, and healthy childrearing. Access to nutrition, reproductive, and child health services is key. Health education and life skills training can encourage youth to delay marriage and use health services. Early child development programs can promote parenting skills. Second-chance services can help young mothers overcome the obstacles of low education and poor employment opportunities.

This chapter looks at age of sexual initiation, contraceptive use, and other factors in the context of general trends on youth pregnancy and family formation. It also touches on the issue of HIV/AIDS infections. The final section raises some questions for a discussion of health and youth policy.

Argentine Youth Are Sexually Initiated at Younger Ages

The mean age of sexual initiation is about 15.5 years for men and 16.2 years for women, with about 70 percent of young men and 55 percent of young women in the YSCS survey sample reporting having been sexually initiated.[56] Table 6.5 presents the

---

56. The YSCS asked all respondents whether they had ever had a sexual relationship and, if they answered affirmatively, at what age it occurred and with whom. These findings should not be interpreted as the average age of the first sexual encounter of a cohort, because these estimates are based on teenagers who have had sexual relations, ignoring those who have not (Contreras and Hakkert 2001).

Table 6.5. Cumulative Percentage of Sexually-initiated Youth, By City of Residence and Gender

By Age	Males				Females			
	GBA	Salta	Neuquén	Posadas	GBA	Salta	Neuquén	Posadas
14	8.9	4.6	5.1	5.2	1.7	0.5	1.4	1.7
15	22.5	15.3	13.0	14.2	8.5	3.3	5.7	5.2
16	41.0	25.7	24.8	38.6	20.7	15.5	19.5	15.0
17	57.7	35.3	46.7	55.4	35.8	21.4	34.1	25.7
18	70.2	55.2	62.6	69.4	54.6	36.7	50.6	47.1
19	83.6	75.3	86.5	82.3	69.4	56.6	72.0	65.4
20	85.0	89.7	90.4	91.1	79.0	68.0	87.5	72.2

Source: Calculations based on YSCS.

cumulative probabilities of sexual initiation until the age of 20 for men and women.[57] A small proportion of males have their sexual debut at even earlier ages: just under 10 percent have their first sexual encounter before age 14. But this proportion more than doubles by age 15 (13–22 percent), increasing to 35–58 percent by the age of 17, and to 75–86 percent by the age of 19. By the time men turn 20, between 85 and 91 percent are sexually initiated. Young men in greater Buenos Aires and Posadas have their first sexual encounter earlier than their peers in Neuquén and Salta. At any given age, the proportion of women who are sexually initiated is lower than the comparable proportion of men. Only a minority of women have their first sexual encounter before age 15 (3–9 percent). This proportion increases to 15–21 percent by the age of 16 and to 37–55 percent by 18. By the time they turn 20, between 68 and 87 percent of women have had their sexual debut. As with men, there are regional differences, with young women in Posadas and Salta reporting a later sexual initiation than their peers in greater Buenos Aires and Neuquén.

---

57. Decrement life tables are useful in estimating the time of sexual initiation since they also contemplate the experience of the youth who had not had sex at the time of the survey. Rates are estimated by dividing the number of individuals making the transition during a particular age by the number of person-years lived during that age interval. Transitional probabilities are estimated by dividing the number of individuals making the transition at a given age by the number of persons who were not sexually initiated at the beginning of that age minus half of the censored cases. Cumulative probabilities at a specific age are estimated as $Qt = Q(t-1) + q(t-1) * \{1-Q(t-1)\}$, where Qt is the cumulative probability of being sexually initiated by the beginning of t years old; Qx(t-1) is the cumulative probability of becoming sexually initiated by the beginning of the t-1 years old; and qx(t-1) is the transitional probability of becoming sexually initiated during the t-1 years old (given that the individual has not have had sexual relationships until that age).

Table 6.6. Discrete Event History Estimates Predicting Sexual Initiation Until Age 19 for Men

Variables	Odds Ratio
Intercept	0.25[a]
Age (tv)	
14 or younger	0.18[a]
15	0.87
16	
17	1.29
18	2.52[a]
19	1.39
City	
Greater Buenos Aires	
Salta	0.69[b]
Neuquén	0.85
Posadas	1.00
Household's bathroom*	
Inadequate bathroom	
Adequate bathroom	0.96
Mother's education	
Incomplete high school or less	0.92
Completed high school or more	
School enrollment (tv)	
Enrolled	
Not enrolled	1.70[a]
Work experience (tv)	
Does not have work experience	
Has work experience	1.90[a]
Tv: time-variant	

*Adequate bathroom refers to having flushing water.
[a]p < .001; [b]p < .05; [c]p < .10.
Source: Calculations based on YSCS.

Leaving school and work experience are significant determinants of sexual initiation among men (Table 6.6).[58] At any given age, men not attending school are 70 percent more likely to have had their sexual debut than those who are attending.[59] Working youth have odds of sexual initiation 90 percent higher than those who do not work. An analysis of an interaction effect between school enrollment and work experience on the probability of being sexually initiated fails to find any significant effect. Those residing in Salta show the lowest rates of sexual initiation, with odds 30 percent lower than those living in greater Buenos Aires. This result suggests that contextual factors have an important influence.

Data further indicate that men's sexual initiation occurs in varied contexts. For almost two-thirds of those living in Salta, Posadas, and Neuquén, sexual initiation occurs with a girlfriend and in the context of a steady relationship. A friend is the second most common sexual partner (31 percent in Salta and about 18–20 percent in Posadas and Neuquén), followed by a sex worker (12–14 percent in Posadas and Neuquén and 3 percent in Salta). Young men living in greater Buenos Aires show a somewhat different pattern: their most frequent partner for sexual initiation is a girlfriend, but

58. In order to identify factors associated with sexual initiation until age 19, a person-year data base is constructed starting at age 11. The model includes age, city of residence, type of bathroom in the household, mother's education, school enrolment, and labor status. To ease interpretation, the effect of each independent variable is exponentiated to indicate the multiplicative effect of each predictor on the odds of sexual initiation. These effects represented in the metric of odds ratio are interpreted as the multiplicative effect of a one-unit change in the dependent variable.

Odds ratios are estimated using a binomial logistic regression model. If the odds ratios are reduced by 1 and multiplied by 100, they indicate the percentage increase (if greater than 1) or decrease (if less than 1) in the rates of sexual initiation associated with each unit of the explanatory variable.

59. Additional models further tested whether there was a differential effect among those not enrolled according to whether they have completed high school (not shown in tables), but no significant differences were found.

this proportion is substantially lower (45 percent). The remaining majority has their sexual initiation in a less steady context: 35 percent with a friend, 9 percent with a sporadic partner, and 8 percent with a sex worker. Those who had their sexual initiation with their girlfriends had a slightly higher mean age at sexual initiation than the rest (15.8 compared to 15.4).

School enrollment has a much stronger effect on postponing sexual initiation among women than among men. The odds of sexual initiation among young women who do not attend school are 2.6 times the odds of those who are attending (Table 6.7). Having work experience hastens sexual initiation for women—women with work experience are 42 percent more likely to have had their sexual initiation than their peers without work experience. Sexual initiation varies by city of residence: young women in Salta and Posadas have a later sexual initiation than their peers in greater Buenos Aires and Neuquén. And contrary to what was observed among men, social background (proxied by type of bathroom and mother's education) is a significant predictor of the timing of sexual initiation among women.

The interaction between school attendance and work experience turned out to be highly significant for women in predicting sexual initiation. Compared with young adolescents enrolled in school who have never worked, young women not attending school (with or without work experience) are 200 percent more likely to be sexually initiated, while young women enrolled at school with work experience are 63 percent more likely (data not shown in tables).

Most young women report having had their sexual initiation with a boyfriend (77–85 percent). Between 10–15 percent of those living in Salta, Neuquén, and Posadas report their husbands as their first sexual partner, although it is not possible to tell whether sexual initiation occurred at the time of marriage or whether the interviewees married their

Table 6.7. Discrete Event History Estimates Predicting Sexual Initiation Until Age 19 for Women

Variables	Odds Ratio
Intercept	0.15[a]
Age (tv)	
14 or younger	0.12[a]
15	1.03
16	
17	2.03[a]
18	2.86[a]
19	2.05[a]
City	
Greater Buenos Aires	
Salta	0.59[a]
Neuquén	0.94
Posadas	0.69[b]
*Household's bathroom**	
Inadequate bathroom	
Adequate bathroom	0.92
Mother's education	
Incomplete high school or less	1.03
Complete high school or more	
School enrollment (tv)	
Enrolled	
Not enrolled	2.58[a]
Work experience (tv)	
Does not have work experience	
Has work experience	1.42[a]
Tv: time-variant	

*Adequate bathroom refers to having flushing water.
[a]$p < .001$; [b]$p < .05$; [c]$p < 0.10$.
Source: Calculations based on YSCS.

Table 6.8. Proportion of Sexually-initiated Women Who Have Used Condoms and the Birth Control Pill (percent)

	Buenos Aires	Salta	Neuquén	Posadas
Condom	85.9	61.6	34.7	55.5
Pill	30.2	31.5	68.0	45.6

Source: Calculations based on YSCS.

first sexual partner. Nonetheless, sexual initiation for these young women occurred in the context of a steady relationship. Only in greater Buenos Aires do 14 percent report having their first sexual relationship with a friend, with the comparable proportion in the other localities between 2–5 percent.

Education Is Important for Increased Contraceptive Use

The Ministry of Health (2003) estimates that 61 percent of young people ages 15–24 use condoms, but in the YSCS sample reported use is much higher. Of sexually initiated men, 90–98 percent reported using contraceptive methods, predominantly the condom. Women also reported a high use of contraception, although less frequent than males. Women in greater Buenos Aires use contraceptives most frequently (87 percent), followed by those in Salta, Neuquén (83 percent), and Posadas (80 percent). Condoms and the pill are the methods most frequently mentioned, with important differences across cities (Table 6.8).

The greater contraceptive use in greater Buenos Aires, particularly of condoms, may be due to more information about contraceptive methods, sexually-transmitted diseases, and easier availability. Youth in greater Buenos Aires may also engage more frequently in casual or nonsteady sexual relationships—research indicates that youth involved in sporadic or nonsteady relationships use condoms more frequently than those in steady relationships (Kornblit and others 2006).

The high use of contraceptives observed in the YSCS sample does not necessarily indicate responsible lifetime behavior toward safe sex. The survey posed the question about contraceptives in a broad manner that did not inquire about whether respondents were sexually active at the time of the survey, when they had their last sexual relationship, or the pattern of contraceptive use over the course of sexually active years. Several studies have shown that while many young men and women do not use any contraception in their first sexual encounter, contraception use increases over the course of their lives. Contraception use is more frequent among the more educated and those enrolled in school, indicating that those with more education have more access to reproductive health and contraceptive information and have higher opportunity costs from unplanned pregnancy (Table 6.9) (Pantelides and Cerrutti 1992; Pantelides, Gelstein, and Infesta 1995; Gogna, Fernández, and Zamberlin 2005).

Three-quarters of young women from more privileged backgrounds report using contraception in all their sexual relations, but only a third of women from lower income groups do so. Of sexually-active youth, 20 percent of those from less privileged backgrounds report never having used contraception. None from higher income groups do so (Geldstein and Pantelides 2001).

Poor Youth Are Most at Risk for Unplanned Pregnancies

Poor youth are the most exposed to the risk of unplanned pregnancies, partly because of lower awareness of contraception. More than 80 percent of adolescent mothers were not using contraception at the time of conception, but only 35 percent cited a desire to become pregnant as the reason (Gogna, Fernández, and Zamberlin 2005). The Northeast and Patagonia—the country's poorest regions—have the highest rates of under-20 fertility (Table 6.10). In contrast, greater Buenos Aires and Cordoba have the lowest rates.

Adolescent mothers tend to have lower educational attainment, higher labor rates, and more limited access to health insurance. Illiterate women are twice as likely as literate women to become mothers as adolescents (Binstock and Pantelides 2005). Enrolling in high school—and staying there—significantly diminishes the chances that an adolescent girl will have children: a recent study found that almost half of teenagers giving birth in public hospitals were dropouts when they became pregnant (Gogna, Fernández, and Zamberlin 2005). Another study shows that adolescent mothers also work more: 36 percent of adolescent mothers work, compared with 21 percent of nonmothers (Binstock and Pantelides 2005). The same study found that only 27 percent of 14–19-year-old mothers have access to medical insurance, compared 53.2 percent among their peers.[60]

Table 6.9. Proportion of Sexually-initiated Women Who Have Used Contraception, By Education and Age Group

Level of Education	Age	
	15–19	20–24
Incomplete high school and not attending	69.4	73.5
Completed high school and attending	83.8	77.8
Completed high school		83.9
Superior		92.5

Source: Calculations based on YSCS.

Table 6.10. Percentage of Live Births to Mothers Below the Age of 20 for Selected Regions in Argentina, 2004

Argentina (total)	14.1
Northeast region	20.9
Corrientes	17.7
Chaco	22.8
Formosa	20.1
Misiones	19.3
Patagonia region	17.0
Chubut	17.4
La Pampa	16.5
Neuquén	16.5
Rio Negro	17.2
Santa Cruz	15.3
Tierra del Fuego	13.4
Center region	12.5
Buenos Aires city	6.1
Greater Buenos Aires	11.9
Cordoba	13.2
Entre Rios	16.4
Santa Fe	16.4

Source: Ministry de Salud (2006).

---

60. Health insurance refers to schemes such as *emergencia médica, plan de salud privado, mutual or obra social*.

Table 6.11. Discrete Event History Estimates Predicting Adolescent Pregnancy

Variables	Odds Ratio
Intercept	0.08[a]
Age at sexual initiation	
15 or younger	
16	0.60
17	0.68
18–19	0.88
Years since first sex (tv)	
1	0.60
2	1.11
3 or more	
City	
Greater Buenos Aires	
Salta	2.42[a]
Neuquén	1.46
Posadas	1.05
Mother's education	
Incomplete high school or less	2.04[a]
Completed high school or more	
Household's bathroom	
Inadequate bathroom	2.18[a]
Adequate bathroom	
School enrollment (tv)	
Enrolled	
Not enrolled	3.16[a]
Work experience (tv)	
Never worked	
Worked	0.90
Person years	922

[a]$p < .001$; [b]$p < .05$; [c]$p < .10$.

Note: A person/year database was constructed following each woman from the age of sexual initiation to the age when she reported her first pregnancy (if it had occurred prior to 20). The dependent variable (pregnancy occurrence) was coded 0 at each age when the woman was not pregnant and 1 at the age of pregnancy (129 women had a pregnancy during adolescence). Women who did not become pregnant before the survey were truncated at the age of the interview (or at 20 for those women 20–24 at the time of the survey). The analysis used a binomial logistic regression. The explanatory variables included in model are age at sexual initiation, years since sexual initiation (time variant), city of residence, mother's education, type of bathroom, type of relationship with first sexual partner, school enrollment (time variant), and work experience (time variant).

Source: Calculations based on YSCS.

One study has found that more than 25 percent of young mothers surveyed had more than one child during adolescence and nearly 8 percent of mothers 18–19-years old had three or more children (Binstock and Pantelides 2005). Gender roles are important in these reproductive decisions (Geldstein and Pantelides 1997). Youth from less privileged backgrounds often view motherhood as the apex of a woman's life. Before pregnancy teenagers from lower income families often lack educational and professional goals, making pregnancy a way to establish an identity, gain social recognition, and transition to adulthood (Zamberlin 2005).

Many teenage mothers do not go through pregnancy alone. Their parents or spouses are often important, but these partnerships are changing. Of mothers under 14, 42 percent report living with their parents. This number increases to 52 percent for those 15–17-years old and to 71 percent those 18–19-years old. More than 50 percent of teenage mothers live with a spouse or consensual partner, but this proportion has declined from 66 percent in 1980. The share of consensual unions has increased compared with that of marriage (Binstock and Pantelides 2005).

Youth parenthood is the result of a complex chain of decisions about sexual activity, contraception, and whether to carry the baby or risk an abortion. Although often not the result of thorough deliberation and adequate information, these decisions are influenced by social, cultural, family, and individual factors (Pantelides and Cerrutti 1992).

Adolescent women whose mothers did not complete high school are

Table 6.12. HIV/AIDS Prevalence Estimates among Youth, Selected Countries (most recent year available)

	Argentina	Brazil	Chile	Uruguay
HIV/AIDS prevalence, 15–24, lower bound, female	0.3	0.4	0.1	0.2
HIV/AIDS prevalence, 15–24, upper bound, female	0.4	0.6	0.2	0.2
HIV/AIDS prevalence, 15–24, lower bound, male	0.7	0.5	0.2	0.4
HIV/AIDS prevalence, 15–24, upper bound, male	1.0	0.8	0.5	0.6
Estimated HIV/AIDS prevalence, 15–24, total	0.6	0.6	0.2	0.4

Source: UNFPA (2005).

twice as likely to become pregnant. Young women living in a poor household are more than twice as likely to become pregnant, even after controlling for the mother's education.[61]

School enrollment, however, is a strong deterrent against adolescent pregnancy: young women out of school are three times more likely to become pregnant (Table 6.11). This effect remains significant even controlling for income. Mother's and daughter's education affect the chances of pregnancy more strongly than age of sexual initiation. It is plausible that these effects are due to better use of contraception by youth with educated mothers, both at sexual initiation and in subsequent relationships.

Salta—where women report later sexual initiation and more often with a husband or live-in partner—has the highest rate of teenage pregnancy, highlighting the importance of beliefs about gender, family, and maternity for youth pregnancy.

High HIV/AIDS Infections May Mean Youth Aren't Aware of Risks

It is estimated that around 120,000 Argentines live with HIV/AIDS, most of whom contracted the infection as adolescents or young adults. The incidence of HIV among the adolescent population is estimated at 0.15 (Ministerio de Salud). While in the past the HIV/AIDS incidence was highest among men, it is now slightly higher among women, suggesting an increase in infections among the heterosexual population (Ministerio de Salud 2005).

The high prevalence of HIV/AIDS among youth in Argentina is a cause for serious concern—100–200 percent higher than in Chile and Uruguay (Table 6.12)—perhaps suggesting that youth are not well informed about the risks of unprotected sex or that effective protection is not easily available to them. The average age for developing AIDS is 31 for men and 28 for women, which means that most were infected during youth (Rubenstein 2003). Poor knowledge of the risks of unprotected sex and the likelihood of contracting HIV/AIDS or other sexually-transmitted diseases can lead young people to make decisions that jeopardize their health.

---

61. Poverty is proxied by the type of household bathroom

Better Family Formation to Benefit Today's Youth—And Tomorrow's

"I no longer fit in my family."

—Anonymous young Argentine

The costs of early childbearing are huge—for youth, the children of young parents, and for society: increased health risks for mothers and children, more school dropouts, fewer job opportunities, lower productivity, and higher poverty. These risks disproportionately affect the most vulnerable: young women from poor households and those who dropout of school are more likely to become pregnant. Adequately preparing young people for family formation and parenthood can decrease fertility and dependency and promote human capital accumulation, productivity gains, and growth and poverty reduction—critical steps in breaking the intergenerational transmission of poverty.

Some questions that may guide policy discussions regarding health and family policy for youth are:

- With reproductive health outcomes closely linked to school attainment, how can youth best be kept in school, particularly for women in poor and rural areas?
- How is youth knowledge about safe sex most effectively enhanced?
- Can condom availability be ensured to sexually active youth and is that a feasible strategy to stem the AIDS epidemic?
- How can consistent contraceptive use be encouraged most effectively among youth?
- Which strategy can best reduce female mortality resulting from abortion?
- Is making emergency contraception available to youth a viable solution for reducing fertility and unwanted pregnancies?
- How can HIV prevention be targeted effectively toward out-of-school youth (given that they are more likely to be sexually active)?
- How can health and pharmaceutical services be made more youth-friendly to increase use of facilities by young people?
- Can media and social marketing campaigns improve young people's knowledge of HIV and train peers to be positive role models?
- How can second-chance health services be expanded to cover all those in need, such as treatment for people who have contracted HIV or sexually-transmitted diseases?

CHAPTER 7

Citizenship and Participation

By Nicola Garcette, Estanislao Gacitúa-Marió, and Alessandra Heinemann

A key element in the development of stable political systems and good governance is the capacity of the state to engage youth and to facilitate their transformation into citizens through political socialization, participation, and education (Beauvais 2001; Fundación Banco de la Provincia de Buenos Aires 2005; Rodríguez 2003; Torney-Purta and others 2001, 2003). Youth participation and civic engagement are important for two reasons. First, the political involvement of young people can influence the political and social development of the societies they live in. Second, youth need to be engaged to develop fully, and a democratic society needs engaged citizens—youth and adults—to prosper. Strengthening youth participation and civic engagement is vital to ensuring the accountability of public institutions and public and private service providers (World Bank 2006b). It is becoming more and more clear that young people need ties and relationships to develop as citizens and become invested in their communities and the larger society. To achieve this, societies must examine how they deal with youth and work toward new norms that include young people in the public life of the community (Rodriguez 2003). Disengaged youth pose a number of risks for societies (see Table 1.2). Low levels of participation are associated with school dropout, crime, and violence.

Young people are assets in development and agents of social and political change (World Bank 2006b). Around the globe they are a major force in democratization processes, peace movements, and anticorruption efforts. They help bring social cohesion and reconciliation to societies affected by conflict. They contribute to building more competitive economies and bringing innovation and flexibility to rapidly changing workplaces. Yet, they often fall through the cracks of public policy and are denied participation in decisionmaking processes (Rodriguez 2003). Young people are often dismissed—either as

75

potential sources of social risk or as too idealistic to make meaningful contributions to politics and social change.

Youth involvement in communities facilitates social change, contributes to improved delivery of services, and increases social accountability—among many other benefits (World Bank 2006b). Most important, by progressively engaging and exercising their citizenship, youth learn to participate in the political system and acquire norms and values that can contribute to the peaceful resolution of conflicts, greater transparency, and improved governance. Low participation, conversely, can result in disenfranchisement, social instability, and decreasing social capital (Ford Foundation 2000; Torney-Purta and others 2003).

In analyzing the progression to adulthood, it is essential to account for how different groups of youth develop identities and transit the path from childhood to adulthood. This transition is linked to the establishment of a new social identity, with new rights and responsibilities that allow young people to enter new relationships and new social roles, roles not previously allowed (Hall and ohters 1999). This chapter focuses on poor and marginal youth in particular.[62]

Two interrelated factors can hinder the transition of young people to adult citizenship: lack of opportunities to express their identity and develop ventures in economic, social, cultural, and personal expression; and scarce opportunities for building social capital and participating in representative institutions and decisionmaking processes. These two factors, though affecting all youth, have a greater impact on poor and vulnerable youth, who have less access to economic, financial, and natural assets.

Argentina's youth are a huge potential resource for development. Voting rates are high, and new social movements incorporating youth groups demonstrate their desire to participate. However, the transition to full citizenship is fraught with potential risks. The consequences of failing to integrate youth are severe—severe for youth and severe for society. This chapter examines the possibilities of citizenship—and the factors hindering young people's transition to its full realization. First, it discusses why youth civic engagement is important and the factors influencing it. It then addresses new forms of youth organization and social mobilization. The next section analyzes crime and violence among Argentine youth, followed by a concluding section that raises some questions to guide the discussion of recommendations for facilitating the transition of youth to responsible citizenship and for improving social cohesion and governance.

Youth and Citizenship—The Challenge of Integration

Social integration for youth means not only total insertion in the workforce and in political, social, and cultural life, but also the smooth transition from dependence on the family—with all that this encompasses—to the independence typical of adult life (Fundación Banco de la Provincia de Buenos Aires 2005). During this process young people enter new legal, cultural, economic, and social arrangements. Yet, social exclusion prevents youth from completing their passage in all these key components of future adult life. Incomplete

---

62. Even among marginal youth differences exist across gender and location (Rodriguez 2003; World Bank 2006b).

education, informal and precarious insertion in the labor force, and an identity established from a marginal or fragmented position in society can undermine the successful integration of youth and their transition to full citizenship.

The transition to citizenship cannot be separated from the other transitions discussed in this report. Unemployment is one of the main risk factors in the transition to adulthood, with spillover effects on citizenship and political participation. The impact of unemployment is most severe for low-income youth and less significant for the wealthiest sectors, in which youth have greater access to resources. Quality of employment is equally important. Temporary and informal employment, more common among youth than among older people, can delay or hinder a successful transition to adulthood (see Chapter 4).

Youth face difficulties in forming households because of financial constraints. Lack of integration, either through the educational system or work, has created isolation and alienation, particularly among the poorest and most marginal youth, who also see their transition truncated in other social dimensions, such as the establishment of independent families (Fundación Banco de la Provincia de Buenos Aires 2005). Youth from less privileged social and economic backgrounds face increasing difficulties in moving out of their parent (or extended) households and establishing their own. They simply cannot afford it.

Without good health, youth cannot hope to become full participants in society. Poor and vulnerable youth have limited access to health and other services. While three of four of those ages 18–25 in the highest wealth quintile have some sort of health coverage, only 38 percent of their peers in the lowest two quintiles do.[63] This is particularly relevant in the case of lack of access to sexual and reproductive public health services, putting poor and marginal youth at risk of unplanned pregnancies and HIV/AIDS (see Chapter 6).

Broad-based Participation Remains a Challenge

Representation and participation are crucial in influencing policymaking and lobbying for adequate services and resources. At the same time, they constitute the mechanisms through which youth learn and transition to adult citizenship. This can be achieved through affiliation to an organization or association, by voting, by influencing policies targeting youth, or by participating in political processes. Too often, however, youth find avenues of participation closed. Even the Internet—despite its promises of inclusion—now further excludes marginalized youth. While affluent youth can easily connect to the World Wide Web, access is often difficult for poor youth, undermining their ability to access information, learn, and participate (Box 7.1).

Limitations of channels and resources to exercise citizenship rights and obligations within the politico-institutional arena pose obstacles to youth in fulfilling their potential as citizens. Low-income youth in Argentina are not well represented in civil and political institutions. While political parties have youth branches, these represent mostly middle class youth (Bermudez 2004; Fundación Banco de la Provincia de Buenos Aires 2005; Petras 2002; Saravi 2004). This lack of representation can contribute to political indifference or discouragement, which can translate into youth feeling incapable of influencing policymaking and demanding basic necessities from the government. Raising youth political

---

63. Data from YSCS.

Box 7.1: Digital Inclusion

The CDI Foundation is a nongovernmental organization with the mission of promoting social inclusion of low-income communities through digital inclusion. Using education and technology as tools for development, CDI believes that learning new technologies contributes to improving living standards, offering youth new opportunities for personal development. The CDI Foundation's objective is to create CDI Centers, which function inside other organizations that work in communities.

In the CDI Centers informatics, social responsibility, and citizenship are integrated through the project methodology: throughout the course, pupils work on a project that offers real solutions to specific community needs.

The CDI Centers work mainly with youth, who cite unemployment as one of their biggest problems. CDI Centers address this difficulty with three basic strategies. First, youth who attend the CDI courses are trained in informatics, a key tool for employment. Second, to broaden the relevance of learning, the CDI Centers emphasize that informatics is nothing more than a tool used in the design and implementation of a project. Third, many of the projects are directly related to employment, and human resources experts advise students on how to build their resumes and how to behave in interviews.

The CDI Centers strive to become as closely involved as possible with communities and the issues they face. One program, developed by the CDI Center "*Del Suburbio*," trained sixteen students who live in especially unfavorable conditions. The CDI Center "*Juntos para Crecer*" obtained a grant from the Security Forum to acquire all the materials needed to train 12 youth in risky situations.

Source: Magdalena Horsburgh, CDI Foundation, Buenos Aires.

participation would create a mechanism for them to voice specific demands and thereby increase government accountability.[64]

Youth participation is low in traditional political processes and outlets such as joining political parties and unions and serving in public office—with the exception of voting, which is high. At the same time, young people have been at the forefront of social change, mobilizing against different regimes, challenging institutions, and embracing new ideas. Many of these mobilizations have taken place in nontraditional and informal ways, outside the institutional shell of formal politics.

According to the World Values Survey, interest in politics has decreased since the 1990s among Argentine youth ages 18–24, and it is low compared with that of other countries.

The YSCS shows that 76.8 percent of those 18–24 years old eligible to vote did so in the last election, compared with 89.2 percent of those 25 and older.[65] Only 28.4 percent of those ages 18–24 participate in organizations, compared with 32.7 percent for those older than 24. Participation varies by income. Among youth voting is most frequent for the top and bottom income quintiles (80-85 percent), falling to 69 percent for the fourth quintile.

---

64. There is increasing evidence from other countries that youth participation increases the accountability of public institutions. Participating youth have a better understanding of administrative, budgeting, and policy issues, increasing their capacity to hold institutions accountable (Guerra 2005; LaCava 2004; Sirriani 2005; Torney-Purta 2001, 2003).

65. While these voting rates appear high compared with the United States and other OECD countries, Argentina enforces compulsory voting for those 18 and older. Although penalties are not strictly enforced, normative pressure raises voting rates.

Participation in organizations is lowest for youth in the bottom quintile, at only 19 percent (Table 7.1).

The low participation in organizations indicates a growing population of disengaged youth.[66] Disengaged from traditional political action and systems of government, some young people are instead relying on direct action over representation. Their episodic manifestations can be a powerful way to address social problems.

Participation in the political system and other social organizations contributes to representative democracy, but direct democracy can continue outside such channels.[67] The economic and political processes that have transpired since 2000, however, lead to apathy among some youth. Youth political participation has grown through informal channels, self-organization, and direct mobilization. Political participation has also been expressed outside the organizational realm through artistic self-expression (graffiti, music, writing).[68]

Youth participate with greater frequency in organizations they trust and when they perceive their interests as represented. Young men are more likely to participate if they attend an educational institution and if they are single, young women if they are single and older. Youth trust in most institutions appears low in the YSCS (Table 7.2). Only educational and church institutions appear to inspire trust.

Table 7.1. Voting Behavior and Participation of Youth 18–24, By Income Quintile

Quintile (5 = wealthiest)	Voted in Last Election (percent)	Participates in an Organization (percent)
5	84.6	28.5
4	75.6	31.8
3	74.5	36.0
2	68.9	25.7
1	80.2	19.1

Source: Calculations based on YSCS.

New Social Movements

Strong social movements have emerged recently in Argentina, most prominently the "*piqueteros*" and neighborhood popular assemblies. The *piqueteros*—most with different organizational experiences as activists in neighborhood associations, soup kitchens, and the like—are a cluster of heterogeneous groups with different goals, politics, and strategies. Collective action—standing up to defend their rights by blockading streets and highways—defines the *piqueteros*. Similarly, in early 2000 neighborhood popular assemblies allowed youth to express their concerns. Remaining autonomous from traditional political parties

---

66. This is consistent with the findings of Lederman (2001), who suggests that social capital in Argentina is low—and youth participation is even lower—because youth are not well integrated in the economy.

67. Voting is not the only or even the primary measure of civic engagement and democratic participation. Civic engagement starts with simple acts that contribute to developing citizenship, such as establishing networks, participating in neighborhood associations, and standing up for the rights of others (Schudson 1999).

68. See Plevin (2004) on youth graffiti (http://www.abroadviewmagazine.com/archives/spring_06/vandals.html) and Pablo Vilas' discussion of Argentina's "Rock Nacional."

Table 7.2. Declared Level of Trust in the Judicial System, By Age and Income Quintile					
	Poorest Quintile	2nd Quintile	3rd Quintile	4th Quintile	Richest Quintile
Youth 18–24					
Very low or low	52.3	46.5	46.5	40.2	50.7
Very high or high	9.8	9.8	17.5	19.2	11.4
Population older than 25					
Very low or low	48.9	39.7	38.8	36.3	41.1
Very high or high	10.8	12.7	15.7	14.9	20.5

Source: Calculations based on YSCS.

and structures, these groups also provided space for workshops, talks, popular education seminars, youth activities, and recreation (Petras 2002).

Youth participation in these movements has become key for expressing new social conflicts of growing complexity—the heterogeneity of poverty and inequality. While the initial force that instigated the *piquetero* movement was workers who had lost their jobs, the movement soon opened to new actors, particularly marginalized youth, who found a space of direct representation and action. Most *piquetero* groups are nonhierarchical. Autonomy and direct democracy are key organizing principles—decisions are made collectively at assemblies.

As the economic crisis escalated the *piquetero* movement expanded throughout the country, reflecting the challenges existing institutions and representative mechanisms faced in dealing with challenges such as youth unemployment, lack of access to housing, and the like (Vommaro 2000). Although youth participation in the *piquetero* movement has fallen, the movement has helped define a new identity for poor urban youth, changing the political consciousness of the poor in general.

The appeal of these movements, particularly for marginalized youth, has been their capacity to organize groups around social exclusion, creating an identity that transcends their lack of formal representation and channels their discontent. Autonomy and horizontal organization define these movements, which are based on interpersonal relations and question the logic of "representation." This perspective was very attractive to groups of youth (students, neighborhoods, street performers, cultural centers, human rights organizations), who found a way of taking action and generating new areas of emancipation. Important segments of the youth population felt that these movements provided a valid tool for expressing their interests (Zibechi 2003).

The impulse of these new movements—and the participation of different segments of youth in them—reflects not only a new cycle of social mobilization but also the marginalized young people's lack of economic opportunities and struggle to make their voices heard. Still on a small scale, these movements represent a new way of generating and exercising citizenship and channeling representation based on direct democracy. While based on the historical memory of the working class, these movements encompass new social actors—and relationships among them—not mediated by state and political institutions.

Crime and Violence—Obstacles to a Successful Transition

Falling victim to crime and violence, or committing criminal and violent acts, can severely affect young people's lives and preclude successful transitions—to work, to healthy adulthood, to parenthood, and to citizenship. Violence is also costly to society. At the individual level, youth who fall victim to violence not only suffer damage to their physical and mental health, but the experience is also likely to affect their academic performance, employability, and productivity. At the macroeconomic level, Lederman (1999) estimates the economic cost of homicides officially recorded in Argentina in 1997 at almost $28 billion for that year alone—and almost $270 billion over the next 25 years (assuming that victims of homicide had earning potential equal to the annual GDP per capita). The cost of violence, however, goes far beyond forgone earnings. It is estimated that that countries in Latin America devote 0.3–5 percent of GDP to treating the health consequences of violence and between 2–9 percent of GDP to judicial and police services (Buvinic and Morrison 2000). Projections estimate the total cost of domestic violence at 2 percent of GDP in Chile (Morrison and Orlando 1999).

Youth violence is not as prevalent or severe in Argentina as in Central America or Brazil (Kuasñosky and Szulik 1996; Rodgers 1999, 2005). However, recent studies suggest that some youth who neither work nor study have socialized into gangs, engaging in different dimensions of illegal or criminal activity.[69] Extremely heterogeneous, these groups have different motivations—some have political overtones, some are concerned mainly with the accumulation of wealth, and others center on identity and social status (Kessler 2005; Kuasñosky and Szulik 1996, 2000). These gangs emphasize both the symbolic aspects of the social exclusion of Argentine youth and their material conditions (Saraví 2004).

The most recent *World Development Report* indicates that the rate of youth incarceration in Argentina is higher than average (World Bank 2006b). The rate of youth incarceration in Argentina is higher than in Perú, Nicaragua, and Bolivia, though lower than in Mexico, Panama, and Chile. Although internationally Argentina has worked to advance human rights for youth, the high incarceration rates indicate that these approaches have not yet fully permeated the juvenile justice system. Argentina has experimented with alternative models of juvenile justice, giving youth educational grants rather than incarcerating them (Muncie 2005; Kellogg Foundation 2006). Existing laws, however, do not clearly distinguish young criminals by the type of offense committed to assess the feasibility of alternative sentencing. As a result, the judicial and penal system remains at best an imperfect system for dealing with the criminal responsibility of juveniles and reintegrating them into society.

Youth is when most criminal careers begin, making a compelling case for focusing crime prevention efforts on youth and offering feasible rehabilitation options to youth who have committed criminal offenses.[70] When caught, however, young offenders are often treated in the same way as adults or dismissed as lost causes. Detention facilities have been

---

69. A recent article by Monte Reel in the *Washington Post* (February 24, 2007) describes alleged links between *barras bravas* and gangs that receive money and jobs from the football clubs to harass other club fans. See also Kessler (2005).

70. See Greenwood (1995) and Levitt and Lochner (2000) for data on the United States; Galiani and others (2006).

found to expose young offenders to additional risks, making repeat-offenses more likely rather than rehabilitating young people to contribute positively to their communities (UN 2006). So, it is efficient to differentiate carefully by the type of criminal and to assess the feasibility of sentencing programs that offer alternatives to incarceration (community service, for example). Not only is incarceration very costly, but alternative sentencing has also proven an efficient way to address the needs of victims and juvenile offenders committing small offenses, benefiting communities as a whole (UNICEF 2004). When youth commit serious crimes, jails should focus on rehabilitating these young people and teaching them skills, which will enable their inclusion in society and the labor market upon release. The private sector should be encouraged to employ these youth as part of corporate social responsibility.

Argentina's homicide rate is at least five times higher than that in France, Italy, and Spain. Although by Latin American standards Argentina's levels of crime and violence are mild, young males have had a disproportionate likelihood in recent years of committing crimes and falling victim to violence. During the past 15 years violent crime has increased by about 200 percent. As a result, insecurity is now a key public concern, and opinion polls show that 50 percent of Argentines perceive insecurity to be on the rise in their neighborhood.[71] While homicide rates in Argentina compare favorably with those in most countries in the region, Chile and Uruguay have lower homicide rates, as do most OECD countries. Recent WHO estimates of homicide rates per 100,000 people for males ages 15–29 were 11.5 in Argentina, 6.7 in Chile, 6 in Uruguay, 2.7 in Italy, 1.5 in Spain, and 0.9 in France (WHO 2002). Data from the Ministry of Justice underscore the centrality of young males in perpetrating crime and violence: males ages 18–20 make up 25 percent of those sentenced for crimes in Argentina (Garcette 2006).

Exposure to violence in youth is closely related to other risk factors that diminish the odds of a young person's successful transition into wholesome and responsible adulthood (see Table 1.2). Cluster analysis based on the YSCS data for four provinces in Argentina reveals that youth who grow up in violent households have higher rates of early sexual initiation and school dropout than their peers from nonviolent households (Figure 7.1). These findings are consistent with research on the United States and Latin America, which has demonstrated that youth at risk of engaging in violent behavior often display other characteristics that can put them at risk: poverty, alcoholism, drug use, mental health problems, abuse, neglect, high-crime neighborhoods, problems in school, school dropout, unemployment, inadequate or inconsistent parenting, inadequate bonding with community institutions, and involvement with delinquent peers (Greenwood 1995, Dowdney 2005). Domestic violence is particularly devastating for women. Projections estimate the total cost of domestic violence at 2 percent of GDP for Chile (Morrison and Orlando 1999). In 1999 women legislators in Argentina played a critical role in ensuring the passage of a law that modified the penal code to define sexual crimes against women and children and toughen the penalties for such acts (UNICEF 2006).

From a policy perspective these trends are cause for concern. Not only do deaths, injuries, and disabilities resulting from crime and violence constitute a serious public

---

71. Gallup data are for 2002. In 1997–2000, 32–39 percent of respondents felt insecurity had grown in their neighborhoods (quoted in Garcette 2006).

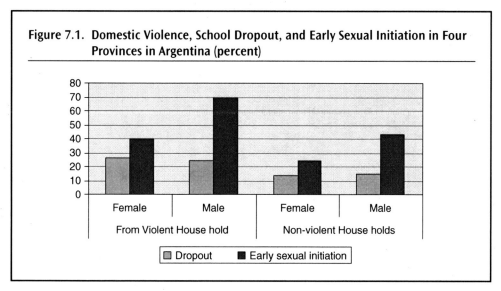

Figure 7.1. **Domestic Violence, School Dropout, and Early Sexual Initiation in Four Provinces in Argentina (percent)**

Source: Calculations from YSCS.

health burden, but the cost of violence also accrues more broadly to society. Violence has been demonstrated to erode human and social capital. It depresses savings and investments. It reduces labor force participation, productivity, and tourism. And it diverts scarce resources to the police, prisons, and courts, reducing growth and development and perpetuating poverty.[72] A holistic and systematic approach to violence control and prevention—targeted at high-risk youth and their families, addressing risk factors at various levels—can reduce violence. There is a growing body of evidence that indicates that youth violence can be prevented and that offenders can be rehabilitated to contribute to their communities.

Crime and Violence Hit Youth Hard

While data collection on crime and violence has improved in Argentina in recent years, the lack of comprehensive victimization surveys for high violence areas precludes thorough analysis of the dynamics of youth violence and the associated risk and protective factors. Since 2002 the Ministry of Justice has reported indictment rates according to the age of the offender, grouping males and females in three brackets: ages 15–17, 18–24, and 25–44 for homicide data, and ages 15–17, 18–21, and 22–44 for property crime data. While this chapter uses indictment rates as a proxy for actual crime and violence levels, it must be noted that they can give only an indication of general patterns of crime and violence.[73]

---

72. See, for example, Ayres (1998) for a thorough discussion of the costs of violence and its impact on development.

73. There are important caveats regarding this data. First, homicide rates are a proxy for violence, but they fail to capture accurately nonfatal types of violence, especially domestic and sexual violence. Second, underreporting is severe. It is estimated that only 33.4 percent of all property crime in the city of Buenos Aires is reported (Kessler 2004).

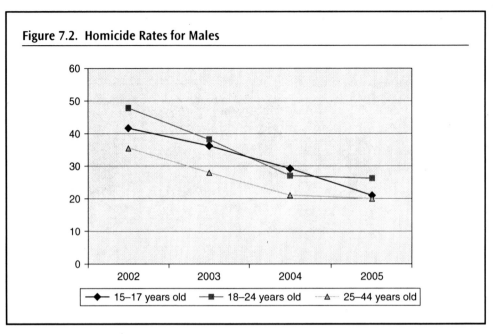

Figure 7.2. Homicide Rates for Males

Note: Rates are per 100,000 people belonging to the same category, 2002–05.
Source: Authors' calculations.

This section presents trends on crime and violence for youth in Argentina based on available data for 2002–05 and the YSCS. It offers some insights into risk factors associated with violent behavior based on panel data, YSCS data, and other sources. The small sample size, however, does not allow robust conclusions. The last section offers some guiding questions for policy discussions.

Young men ages 18–24 were the most likely to commit homicide over the past four years, though there was an overall decline in homicides (Figure 7.2). Homicide rates declined by about 45 percent for men ages 18–24 and 25–44 and by 50 percent for 15–17-year-olds. Young men ages 18–24 were the most indicted during 2002–05, accounting for 33 percent of male homicide indictments—and they were 14 times more likely than women of the same age to be indicted. Their indictment rate was 30 percent higher than that of adults and 10 percent higher than that of minors.[74] Homicide indictment rates increased slightly for 18–24-year-olds and adult men during 2002–05. For minors homicide indictments increased by 30 percent in 2002–04 and then decreased by 25 percent in 2005.

Homicide rates for young women ages 18–24 fell by 46 percent. For females younger than 18 and those older than 25, the homicide rate increased by 10 percent (Figure 7.3). Among females, 15–17-year-olds accounted for 11 percent of those indicted for homicide, while 18–24-year-olds accounted for 30 percent.

Minors have the highest victimization rates among females, but adults have the highest victimization rates among males. For homicide minors have the highest victimization

74. "Adult" in this section refers to people older than 25, and "minor" refers to 15–17-year-olds.

Figure 7.3. Homicide Rates for Females

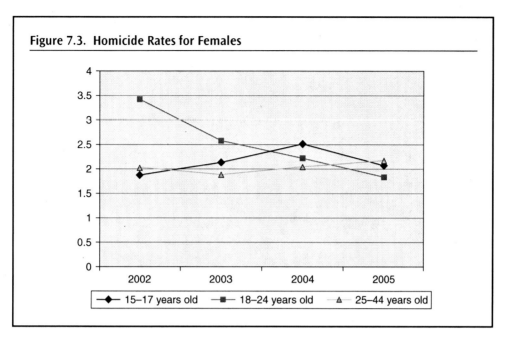

Note: Rates are per 100,000 people belonging to the same category, 2002–05.
Source: Authors' calculations.

rates among females, with minors accounting for 16 percent of female homicide victims but only 5 percent of the total female population (Figure 7.5). Young women ages 18–24 accounted for 14 percent of female homicide victims, females ages 25–44 for 70 percent. But for males the adult victimization rate was 15 percent higher than that of 18–24-year-olds and 25 percent higher than that of 15–17-year-olds (Figure 7.4). Adult men accounted for 63 percent of male homicide victims from 2002 to 2005, compared with 26 percent for 18–24-year-olds and 10 percent for 15–17-year-olds—shares that remained remarkably stable over the last four years. The homicide victimization rate has always been higher for men than for women, whatever the age category. In particular, the homicide victimization rate was nearly 18 times higher for 18–24-year-old men than for women of the same age over 2002–05.

While 18–20-year-olds accounted for 25 percent of prison sentences in Argentina since 2002, the 15–17 group accounted for only 1 percent.[75] The adult share of sentences is predominant. Youth have also been the most indicted for property crimes, though again overall property crime fell since 2002. Those 15–17 years old accounted for 26 percent of indictments for theft and 25 percent for robbery. Youth ages 18–21 made up 23 percent of indictments for theft and 27 percent for robbery.

Descriptive data from the YSCS offers a context-specific snapshot of youth crime and victimization for Buenos Aires, Misiones, Salta, and Neuquén, where about 8 percent of young respondents reported suffering from a violent act at home. Perhaps surprisingly, domestic violence seems to affect young men and women in the same proportions. The

---

75. Age is unknown in 40 percent of the sentences during the past four years.

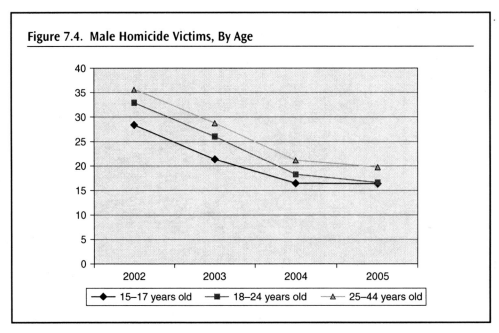

Figure 7.4. Male Homicide Victims, By Age

Note: Rates are per 100,000 people belonging to the same category, 2002–05.
Source: Authors' calculations.

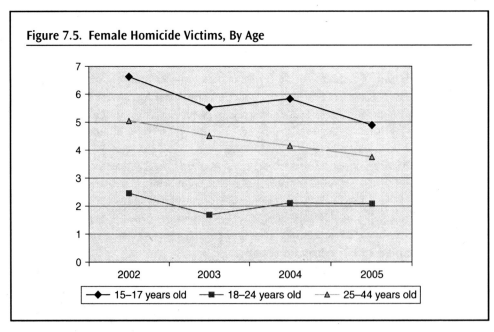

Figure 7.5. Female Homicide Victims, By Age

Note: Rates are per 100,000 people belonging to the same category, 2002–05.
Source: Authors' calculations.

father was reported to be the assailant in 56 percent of cases—and in 65 percent of the cases for young women. The proportion of youth who reported feeling unsafe in their neighborhood is high (65 percent), but close to the proportion of adults (67 percent). For property crime 21 percent of young people reported being victimized during the previous year. Burglaries were reported by 10 percent of young people and robberies by 9 percent. Only 2 percent reported thefts.

Nearly half of young people reported witnessing a group assaulting another group in the neighborhood during the past 12 months. Half of those who witnessed these assaults reported that both groups were made up of young people. About 60 percent of them reported that either the assailant or the victim group was made up of young people. Among young men 11 percent declared having been involved in a violent assault during previous month, compared with only 4 percent of young women. Asked about the previous year, 29 percent of young men declared that they were the victim of a violent act, compared with 15 percent of young women.

Risk Factors—Preliminary Findings

As mentioned previously, the absence of comprehensive data on victimization and individual characteristics of young offenders precludes thorough analysis of the dynamics of youth violence and the risk factors associated with it. This section offers a preliminary analysis of risk factors, based first on panel data (by constructing economic variables using the Permanent Household Survey and demographic variables using the 2001 census) and second on micro data from the YSCS. That the panel data covers only four years is a significant drawback. Female homicides were so rare in some provinces that regressions are restricted to males and the whole population. Furthermore, the analysis excludes variables such as provincial police expenditure, since these data were not available. The proxy variables for crime rates have been constructed from indictment rates, which depend in large measure on police efficiency.

The econometric analysis offers only inconclusive results regarding the effect of economic and social variables on homicide victimization. Findings suggest that high unemployment leads to more homicides for minors, but it must be noted that other studies have not found this to be the case. Among those ages 18–24, however, high unemployment exhibits a negative, but slightly significant, effect on homicide victimization. But male-specific regressions fail to replicate these results.

Participation exerts a strong negative effect on the homicide victimization rate of males younger than 18. The proportion of people who have completed only primary school has a strong significant and positive effect on the homicide victimization rate whatever the age category. In contrast, secondary school achievement has no significant effect on any of the youth and adult homicide rates. Population density has a significant negative effect on the homicide rate for those ages 18–24 in all regressions.

In some regressions only population density and unemployment rates exhibit a significant effect on homicide rates. But the coefficient sign is surprising for both variables. Areas with higher population density had lower homicide rates for minors, and areas with higher unemployment had lower homicide rates for those 18–24-years old. Regressions considering only males lead to the same results.

An analysis of risk factors based on the YSCS data finds that, when compared with nonvictims, youth victims of violent crime and youth involved in violent assault are more likely to belong to the poorest quintiles, to be male, to use alcohol and drugs, and to live in a broken family and with an adult using drugs (Table 7.1). Youth from the poorest quintiles living in broken families are also more likely to suffer from domestic violence. Perhaps surprisingly, youth belonging to an organization also seem more likely to be the victim of a property crime or a violent crime. Youth victims of property crime are less likely to belong to the richest quintile and to have a mother who completed university, but more likely to consume drugs and to live with an adult who uses drugs.

Property crimes and homicides are concentrated in Buenos Aires—17 percent of thefts, 27 percent of robberies, 57 percent of car thefts, 65 percent of car robberies, and 47 percent of homicides took place in Buenos Aires in 2002–05 (Garcette 2006). Crime and violence in Argentina tend to occur in places with higher population density.

Other analyses of risk factors for crime and violence indicate correlations between youth crime and violence and high youth unemployment rates. Between 1990 and 2002 unemployment increased by 120 percent for the labor force and by 160 percent for youth. The deterioration of the labor market and the extreme increases in youth unemployment in 1990–2002 are positively correlated with crime, suggesting that crime rates increase with unemployment. Cerro and Meloni (2000) conclude that a 10 percent rise in unemployment increases the crime rate in Argentina by 1.8 percent (Cerro and Meloni 2000). Youth unemployment reached 26.3 percent (718,000 people) in 2005, 40 percent of the total unemployed population.[76] Kessler (2005) argues that the instability of the labor market during the last few years, among other factors, led youth to combine legal and illegal activities to survive.[77] In Buenos Aires 58 percent of youth younger than 18 involved in crime are still in school (Kessler 2003). Studies for other countries, however, conclude that young offenders are often school dropouts. So, though efforts to educate the young may not reduce crime and violence levels immediately, they can eventually have a significant impact (Dowdney 2004; FLL 1998).

There is also evidence associating growing inequality with higher homicide and property crime rates (Fajnzylber, Lederman, and Loayza 1998, 2000, 2002a, 2002b). Garcette (2005) links the increase in property crime in Argentina to the levels of income inequality (as measured by the Gini coefficient, which has risen 12 percent since 1996), concluding that income inequality can explain 10–15 percent of the rise in property crime in 1992–2002. A study of the determinants of entry into criminal activities by Galiani, Rossi, and Schargrodsky (2006) find that military service increases the likelihood of developing a criminal record later (particularly for property and weapon crimes).

Actions to Promote Citizenship and Reduce Crime and Violence

Easing the transition of poor and marginal youth to full citizenship requires the inclusion of marginalized youth through capacity building, social support, and economic, social, and political empowerment (LaCava and others 2004). It is important that policies and programs

---

76. Ministerio de Trabajo (2005), quoted in Carlsson (2006).
77. Kessler (2005), quoted in Carlsson (2006).

recognize heterogeneity among youth and also be multisectoral and comprehensive—citizenship development is inseparable from other transitions to the workforce, to a healthy life, and to parenthood (for recommendations on these dimensions, see Chapter 8).

Empowered youth can change society for the better—but only if they have the necessary political, social, and human capital. Without these, youth may fall into economic, social, and psychological isolation. Policies for youth inclusion should begin by expanding their economic opportunities, the key to lowering social risks and raising engagement as productive adults.

Strengthening networks and social bonds among youth is important. Facilitating communications and access to information and technology can enhance trust, understanding, and participation. Building horizontal social capital, however, is not sufficient. Increasing participation and promoting interactions among youth from different economic and social backgrounds can increase trust, develop partnerships for collective decisionmaking, and create opportunities for teaching and learning (Box 7.2).

Facilitating the engagement of youth in community development and transferring resources and decisionmaking responsibilities to youth has proven effective. Bringing youth into community activities—from AIDS campaigns to local planning—forges a common vision and sense of identity, increasing solidarity and trust among participants, including youth and other social groups. Promoting youth participation gives them a voice to articulate their needs and contribute to the decisionmaking process. For example, participatory planning (such as participatory budgeting in Brazil) increases youth understanding of civic engagement and key policy instruments. By delegating responsibilities to other members of the group, these mechanisms foster trust in processes and institutions (Guerra 2002).

Building the capacity of state institutions to address youth issues and facilitate youth participation in policymaking is another challenge. While participation at the local level is needed, youth engagement in higher levels of policymaking can also be valuable. Enhancing the capacity of youth and state institutions increases the relevance and quality of youth participation, enabling youth to negotiate with, influence, control, and hold accountable the institutions that affect their lives.

Fostering youth political participation as a multidimensional process is a final challenge. While political participation can be channeled through prescribed political processes and institutions (voting in elections, standing for public office), youth political participation can also be encouraged through other mechanisms, such as consultations organized by ministries and agencies addressing youth concerns. Recent experience indicates that political parties and unions are not the only ways of expressing class and group interests. Facilitating membership in social and civic organizations (student councils, neighborhood associations) could provide a valuable avenue for actions that will foster the capacity of youth to build constituencies, generate resources, and express their views.

All these policy directions require awareness of the different cleavages among youth audiences (based on gender, socioeconomic status, and location). For all of these groups, the youth transition to adult citizenship in Argentina has been prolonged—especially for the poorest youth, who face increasing difficulties in finding a stable job, establishing an independent family, and participating in society.

Failing to promote youth inclusion has devastating effects—perhaps none greater than crime and violence. Although good data on youth crime is in short supply, it is appears that

---

Box 7.2: Monitoring and Evaluation among Youth NGOs—Youth As Key Actors at Each Step

The "Monitoring innovative youth programs in the Southern Cone" project supported nongovernmental organizations working with youth by improving the implementation of their programs. The project, conceived as a training/action process, targeted 20 young leaders from Argentina, Chile, Uruguay, and Paraguay and helped them develop project monitoring skills. Designed by World Bank staff and Fundación SES (an Argentine nongovernmental organization with a long history working on youth issues), it continued the work of the "Southern Cone development marketplace" or "Feria del Desarrollo," which provided competitive funding to nongovernmental organizations to implement innovative youth programs. After receiving training, the young leaders monitored (or "accompanied") the implementation of one of the Feria-awarded projects.

The project achieved its objectives and had many positive effects. Monitored or accompanied organizations gained an increased awareness of the importance of monitoring and systematization. Many of them did not monitor their projects before and have started to do so, leading to better implementation of their programs. Moreover, the project has strengthened the network of young leaders committed to youth development issues. Indeed, all youth participating in the monitoring established working agreements with the accompanied nongovernmental organizations to continue working after the project ended. The project's focus on youth as key actors at each step of the project cycle—design, implementation, evaluation, and dissemination—was key to its success.

Project design was innovative. Departing from the previous experiences of the young leaders, the methodology for monitoring and accompanying the projects was built through a participatory method. Using a series of popular educational techniques, the group of young leaders proposed dimensions and aspects for examination during the process. They also organized the sequence and content of questions to be asked at each of the project visits. Based on the youth proposals, Fundación SES designed the instruments applied during the monitoring and accompanying. This participatory design was crucial to smooth application of the methodology: the youth felt confident applying an instrument that they had developed.

The monitoring and accompanying was conducted by the youth. They visited the projects, gathered information, provided feedback to the organizations, and wrote the monitoring reports. But the accompanying process was more than just data gathering. It was a teaching and learning process, in which the two parties benefited from the exchange. To support that process, it was suggested that the youth work in pairs, allowing them to discuss doubts, observations, and recommendations. The youth were also the main actors during project evaluation. They participated in a two day project in which monitoring results were shared, methodology assessed, project objectives analyzed, and the role of SES evaluated.

Giving youth a central role in the project cycle does not mean that they worked alone. The "lessons learned" from the project suggest that the most successful monitoring and accompanying experiences involved an adult from the youth's home organization providing the youth with support and orientation in conducting their work. This relationship was also important in establishing working agreements between the two nongovernmental organizations—the young person's home organization and the one the young person accompanied or monitored.

The youth are currently drafting a publication to communicate the project experience and disseminate a tested methodology designed and used by youth. They are also in charge of designing the publication and distribution strategy, which will particularly target grassroots organizations working with youth.

Source: Marisa Miodosky.

risk factors for crime often overlap with those for other difficulties youth face: poverty, unemployment, broken families, and substance abuse.

To address the threat of crime and violence to individual lives, public security, and development, the following questions could be considered:

■ How can cooperation between local law enforcement and the Ministry of Justice be improved to assess the feasibility of programs to improve police-community relations (such as community policing in high crime neighborhoods)?

■ How can programs such as community justice schemes, graduated sanctions, and rehabilitation be tested for effectiveness and potentially expanded?

■ How can the quality of data available on the prevalence of specific types of youth crime and violence be improved to allow for a more thorough analysis of the issues and to better inform policy decisions?

■ How can the infrastructure of communities to provide basic services, maintain public order, and build social capital, especially in marginalized communities, be strengthened most effectively—while maintaining a focus on youth and their families?

■ Is social marketing a viable means to bolster antiviolence messages?

■ How can violence in the home be reduced and the capacity of parents to be responsible be enhanced most effectively?

■ How can life skills programs be adapted to teach youth appropriate decisionmaking and problem-solving skills from an early age?

CHAPTER 8

Youth Policy Directions To Reduce Youth At Risk

By Juan Felipe Sánchez

"I'd like to participate in forums where concrete public policies can be discussed. Not a very political forum, not in a partisan environment, but rather to discuss more concrete public policies."

—Carolina, 24 years old, studies and works for a nongovernmental
organization, city of Buenos Aires.

Argentina has made tremendous progress in providing basic education and healthcare, especially for children—building a foundation of basic skills and well-being. However, young people must still make a successful transition to adulthood, which requires accessing and completing quality higher education; adjusting to reproductive roles and healthy behaviors; building assets for family life; preparing for the demands of more complex job markets; and becoming capable and participating citizens. Tapping the potential of its young population—specifically its at-risk youth—and investing heavily in human capital formation will allow Argentina to improve economic growth, reduce poverty, and build a more secure society.

Realizing the Benefits of the Demographic Dividend

As seen in the initial chapters, 46 percent of youth ages 15–24 are at some form of risk. Today, too many Argentine youth:

- Live in poverty, with no hope of escaping the poverty trap.
- Lack access to quality—and relevant—secondary and tertiary education; when they do have access, many are not able to complete their education.

- Enter the labor market too early, are unable to find a job, are employed under very difficult circumstances, have lower wages than adults, or cannot stay employed for long.
- Engage in risky behaviors and suffer the consequences of poor choices (early pregnancy, HIV/AIDS, violence, crime, substance abuse).
- Do not feel empowered and perceive a need for a greater voice to contribute to local and national development.

The present youth cohort is Argentina's largest population group. Together with the next generation of children, they will influence the economy, the social fabric, and the politics of the country for at least the next 40 years. By investing in youth now, the country will reap the benefit of this demographic window of opportunity—before rapid aging of the population results in more costly trade-offs between the needs of the young and those of the elderly.

Investing more effectively in its young population will enable Argentina to build a stronger base for better economic growth and security. To achieve this goal, it is necessary to provide quality secondary and tertiary education and to address health threats to youth, such as sexually-transmitted diseases, alcohol, tobacco and drug use, traffic accidents, and violence. For youth who engage in risky behaviors and suffer the consequences of poor choices, second chance programs can help them gain necessary skills and retake their place in society. Labor market reforms are necessary to better accommodate new young entrants and to improve working conditions.

Youth-focused policies must be consistent with national priorities. A more effective cross-sector implementation capacity needs to be in place (with clear coordination structures, implementation mandates and collaborative arrangements, effective youth participation and engagement, and quality monitoring and evaluation).

The cost of not investing in youth is staggering: high unemployment, higher health and social welfare costs, insecurity, and lower economic growth. It is urgent, then, to recognize youth as an asset and invest in them accordingly. Youth constitute a positive force for change (Box 8.1). Investing in Argentina's young people is a necessary and cost-effective way to address youth vulnerability, reduce poverty, and benefit society as a whole.

Box 8.1: Youth Are an Asset to Society

Healthy, educated, engaged, employed, and productive youth are key to breaking the inter-generational cycle of poverty, achieving sustained growth, and building security. When given a chance to participate and contribute, the young may provide much-needed innovation and play a catalytic role in promoting democracy and economic growth; they can create enterprises and generate employment, increase incomes and help connect the country to the rest of the world; they can help younger children—and whole communities—to develop; and they can contribute to slowing the AIDS pandemic and conserving the environment with responsibility.

Source: World Bank (2005a).

Achieving a More Effective Mix of Youth Policies

Because youth respond to their environment, it is sensible to focus on getting the environment right by combating risk factors and promoting protective factors. A number of evaluated programs show that these goals can be achieved even under tight fiscal constraints, for instance by expanding existing early childhood development and gearing the school environment toward lifelong learning and citizenship. Targeting poor youth is essential for maximum effectiveness (McGinnis 2007).

A mixed portfolio of programs and interventions, some specific to youth and some more broadly focused, is required to achieve a balance between short-run targeting of those already suffering negative consequences of risky behaviors—such as through second chance programs and rehabilitation for youth already "stuck"—and long-run prevention to keep other youth from engaging in risky behaviors and to develop their potential (McGinnis 2007).

Focusing policies and programs on the individual (improving life skills, self-esteem), on key relationships (parents, caregivers, peers), on communities (schools, neighborhoods, police), and on societal laws, institutions, and norms provides the greatest chance to reduce the numbers of youth at risk over the long term.

Specific recommendations will be developed during consultations with government counterparts and youth. However, a basic strategy should consider:

- Investing earlier in life and expanding youth opportunities.
- Targeting at-risk youth more effectively.
- Influencing policies that affect youth but that are not youth-specific.
- Engaging youth for better accountability and governance.
- Making public policy work for youth.

These strategic areas for consideration are presented in the following sections.

Investing Earlier in Life and Expanding Youth Opportunities

Prevention strategies and programs are effective not only in developing the potential of young people, but also in addressing both early and late onset of risky behaviors. Improving and expanding existing interventions will broaden opportunities for young people to develop their human capital. This range of policies will aim to have: i) children entering adolescence with basic skills for learning and practical living; ii) young people entering the labor force at the right time, under the right conditions, and with the relevant skills; and iii) young people becoming capable decisionmaking agents.

Consideration should be given to policies and interventions that have proven to work, that promote youth development, and that prevent disadvantaged youth from becoming at-risk. This report recommends that the following programs be given greater consideration.

Scaling up early child development programs to reach most children 0–3 years of age. Early child development programs are one of the most cost-effective ways to build the human capital of the country and prevent risky behaviors in youth (Young 2002; World Bank 2006b). They have a substantial impact on reducing inequalities in education, earnings, health, crime, and violence over a lifetime. When well targeted to the poor and focused on adequate nutritional supplementation, psychosocial stimulation, and parenting and child-care skills, these programs can have important long-term impacts on reducing the risk of early pregnancy, criminal activity, violence, and substance abuse as young people move into their adolescent and young adult years. The long-term effects of these programs also reduce the costs to society of expensive remedial approaches (dealing with repetition or school dropouts and incarceration and rehabilitation programs).

Early child development programs can:

- Provide quality early childhood interventions—with a focus on children 0–3 years of age—and offer parental education and support activities. Early child development can be delivered either through centers or home-based programs. In either case, parents and communities need to be involved.
- Develop parenting skills to prevent child abuse during critical formative years. Abuse can manifest itself internally through depression and outwardly through substance abuse and delinquency. To prevent these negative pathways—with their subsequent high cost for society—it is important to provide support services, coaching, and stress prevention for at-risk parents, who are probably young people themselves.
- Identify problem behaviors early in schools, providing adequate support before these children turn into troubled adolescents.

Improving education so that young people are able to complete secondary school and have better basic skills for further learning, job placement, and practical living. Consideration could be given to:

- Expanding access to a more diverse and flexible upper-secondary and tertiary education system, reorienting curricula so that young people learn practical, relevant job skills (information technology, languages) and life skills (problem solving, collaborative/team work), while creating stronger connections between school and work.
- Evaluating the benefits of repetition against preventive and supportive actions that could have an impact on future positive education outcomes (especially in grades 1–4) and avoiding the creation of incentives that reinforce underachievement (in programs such as the National Scholarship for Students or in prospective conditional cash transfer programs).
- Adapting classes, teaching methods, and materials to the age of pupils and addressing age distortion issues.
- Providing incentive schemes for teachers and administrators.
- Increasing access to books in schools.
- Enhancing parental involvement in children's education.
- Instituting loans or scholarships targeted to deserving students in rural and low-income urban settings.
- Using conditional cash transfers as a key complement for ensuring that disadvantaged youth stay in school (see recommendations on conditional cash transfers below).

Making better information available to young people to help them make the right decisions regarding their health and life choices. Efforts must go beyond mere dissemination of information to build young people's capacity to change attitudes and behaviors and make the right choices (about their health, work, relations, and life in general). Among the recommended interventions are:

- Implementing at all schools: i) a universal curriculum-based HIV and sex education program to reduce risky sexual behaviors; ii) life-skills training to provide self-management and social skills; iii) information on and skills for making informed choices about substance abuse, violence, conflict, and crime prevention.
- Using local and national media to increase exposure to specific social marketing messages and to reduce exposure to negative behaviors.
- Targeting risk prevention messages at schools and in the media to appropriate ages, sexual experience, and culture.

Targeting At-risk Youth More Effectively

Improving and expanding policies that address risk and protective factors should be a priority, with a focus on providing second chances (or in some cases rehabilitation) to youth already at some form of risk—moving away from zero tolerance (or *mano dura*) and toward comprehensive youth development (Box 8.2). The goal of these efforts is to significantly reduce the number of youth at some form of risk (currently 46 percent), helping them access services that safeguard and develop their human capital, reintegrating into society youth who have lost hope, and improving their decisionmaking capabilities to maximize their well-being.

Box 8.2: Interventions for Youth at Risk That Don't Work

- *"Mano dura":* Harsh police measures, incarceration without rehabilitation, trying youth in adult courts.
- *Nonpromotion to succeeding grades:* Holding underperforming youth back in grades or promoting them without support.
- *Traditional vocational training:* Not very effective when using outdated curricula or if training does not have a connection to employers and labor market demand.
- *Traditional youth centers:* Too much emphasis is given to infrastructure rather than to sustainable, youth-focused programming.
- *Shock programs for violence and drug prevention:* Short-term, nonvoluntary, harsh, violence/drug prevention programs.
- *Boot camp:* Shows no significant effects on recidivism, and youth might be exposed to other delinquent youth, possibly reinforcing delinquent behavior.
- *Gun buybacks:* Expensive strategy that consistently shows no effect on gun violence. Firearm training and mandatory gun ownership have also demonstrated no significant effects on reducing violence and crime.

Source: World Bank (forthcoming).

Consideration should be given to policies and interventions that have proven to be more effective and that are recommended for youth who have dropped out of school, are more difficult to reach, and are significantly more at risk of suffering negative outcomes (World Bank 2005a, 2006b, 2008; World Bank Institute 2005).

Scaling up cash transfer programs for disadvantaged youth, conditional on completing secondary school and reducing specific risky behaviors. Conditional cash transfers programs (such as Mexico's Oportunidades Program) that target at-risk youth are showing strong positive effects on the 12–18 age group, helping to preserve investments made at younger ages while improving their prospects (World Bank 2008). Consideration should be given to the possibility of expanding programs that already demand some accountability (see appendix VIII), which could form the basis of an expanded, cross-sector, youth-focused conditional cash transfer program. Among specific components could be:

- Individual learning accounts.
- Targeted financial assistance for tertiary education (a mixture of loans and grants).
- School-based career counseling.
- Targeted scholarships based on merit and need for poor students in secondary schools in rural and urban settings.

Establishing equivalence degree programs that are recognized by the formal education system for over-age youth. Consideration might be given to establishing more flexible opportunities to obtain formal primary, secondary, and tertiary education degrees through quality equivalence programs. Certified degrees increase the chances that employers will provide job opportunities for young people. Program designs should:

- Link with preventive approaches that help reduce repetition in earlier years.
- Provide flexible schedules, practical curricula, and age-specific instruction methods.
- Forge strong links with the formal education system, both for the sake of ensuring equivalency degrees and for maximizing public infrastructure.
- Build relations with potential employers.

Investing in youth service programs. Actively engaging young people in the delivery of public services and public works—especially at the neighborhood/community level—is a way to help young people acquire the experience, knowledge, and values necessary for transitioning to a life of productive employment and engaged citizenship. These programs are most effective for youth in poor rural and urban settings. They can serve as a tool for on-the-job training and for acquiring practical life skills. Youth service programs can provide community childcare, provide basic healthcare services, build sustainable and affordable housing, improve literacy adult rates, and protect the environment (World Bank 2006a).

Supporting after school activities, parent-family involvement, and mentoring services. Interventions in this area might consider expanding:

- Healthy, protective parent/adult—youth interactions—emphasizing parenting skills, managing conflict and family relations, and facilitating family involvement to help reduce domestic violence, substance abuse, school dropout, association with delinquent peers, and trouble with the justice system.

■ After-school activities. Providing supervised after-school activities with both an academic and fun focus can have a positive impact on a range of important skills and behaviors and help young people use their time more positively (World Bank 2008). These programs should serve low-income families, use existing infrastructure as much as possible, and offer a broad range of age-specific, interesting activities.

■ Mentoring services matching the most disadvantaged youth with a caring adult in a one-on-one mentoring relationship will help at-risk youth make proper decisions when facing difficult situations. To be successful, these programs must have a developmental focus, offering training for the mentors, structured activities, expectations of frequent contact, and close monitoring of overall implementation.

Scaling up internships and training for job and life skills. Improving employment prospects for youth at risk requires training programs that offer them a comprehensive package of training in both professional and life skills, followed by workplace internships (World Bank 2008; McGInnis 2007). To be effective, these programs should:

■ Be demand-driven, providing internships with diverse employers.
■ Link employers with training institutes.
■ Include life-skills training.
■ Connect with other second chance education programs that complement technical and on-the-job training (equivalency or evening classes).
■ Use multi-stakeholder collaborations, partnering for sustainability.
■ Measure results on youth development.

Scaling up employment services targeted to at-risk youth. Consideration might be given to addressing the constraints of imperfect information in the labor market (World Bank 2008):

■ Enhancing intermediary services in the labor market, including greater use of the Internet, institutional networking, and more interaction with employers.
■ Targeting at-risk youth, who often lack access to the Internet and depend on informal networks of information to learn about job opportunities.
■ Equating program success with sustained job placement rates, reaching out to the most disadvantaged youth, and emphasizing better performance.
■ Using nongovernmental organizations, youth organizations, and private sector operators to more effectively link training institutions, occupation schools, secondary schools, and potential employers

Institutions and programs targeting at-risk youth should make assets and services more accessible to disadvantaged youth. Interventions, practices, and incentives that affect their internal behavior should be more responsive to youth priorities and concerns. In this sense, consideration should be given to carrying out in-depth institutional analyses to assess how different programs and interventions are reaching at-risk youth.

Influencing Policies That Are Not Youth-specific

Many policies have an important impact on youth—even if youth are not the primary target—because they focus on the broader context and community factors affecting youth. These efforts require strong cross-sector collaboration among multiple stake-holders. Consideration might be given to:

Promoting reforms that broaden labor market opportunities for youth and improve their job conditions. Broad labor market reforms that balance job protection with the flexibility needed to encourage job creation are needed. One possibility is a gradual approach that deemphasizes a segmented labor market for different age groups, in which protection gradually increases as worker's tenure rises.[78] Improving conditions in the informal sector and facilitating transition to formal economic activities is also important.

Focusing micro-credit/micro-enterprise programs on youth. These programs maximize financial and technical resources to create economic opportunities and generate employment for youth—especially for young female household heads—through:

- Expanding formal bank and financial services for the poor in urban and rural settings—such as small-scale savings and loans schemes—to facilitate incorporating young people into formal financial systems.
- Channeling financial, material, and technical resources toward low-income communities with large numbers of young people to increase access to housing and sustainable employment.

Strengthening police and justice system responses to youth issues. Preventing youth crime and violence requires reforming criminal and juvenile justice systems to reflect the age-specific needs and priorities of the young. Consideration should be given to policies that also enhance the capacity of communities to provide viable solutions to conflict and interpersonal problems in the family. Some examples of interventions in this area are:

- Enhancing family and specialized youth courts to more effectively accommodate youth cases. These services should be closer to families, centrally located within low-income neighborhoods or rural communities.
- Increasing the police and the military's understanding of and capacity to act on age-specific issues and priorities of the young population, including being aware of and having the skills to implement the Rights of the Child Convention.
- Separating juvenile delinquents from adults in jails.
- Having a system of graduated sanctions that fit the offense and encompass a range of nonresidential and residential alternatives for young offenders.

Building safe neighborhoods and communities. Programs that combine improved urban designs, social services, and community policing to create safer communities must also target young people. These programs can have positive effects on basic services at the neighborhood/community level (early child development/education, health,

---

78. Such a program is being explored in France, as suggested by World Bank (2006b).

water/sanitation/hygiene) and on security and safety, helping prevent risky youth behavior and promoting youth development. Some potential areas for enhancement are:

- Age-specific/safe urban spaces (public spaces, parks, pathways/walkways).
- Road safety/traffic control.
- Location/delivery of youth-friendly social services in neighborhoods (early child development centers, basic health facilities, Internet centers, sports facilities).
- Safe water and sanitation, hygiene campaigns, waste management/recycling.
- Control of public spaces, safe roads/pathways to schools, public lighting, community policing, and neighborhood police facilities.

Limiting the availability of alcohol and tobacco. Policies that reduce youth access to alcohol can have an important impact across a range of negative outcomes (World Bank 2008). Consideration might be given to:

- Restricting sales can be accomplished by limiting hours of operation, prohibiting liquor retail near schools, enforcing minimum age purchasing laws, and prohibiting alcohol use at community and sports events or in public areas. For these measures to be effective there has to be a credible threat of sanction.
- Increasing prices through taxation will help reduce overall consumption of alcohol and tobacco, especially among youth, who are very price-sensitive.

Including youth-directed messages in antiviolence/conflict prevention campaigns. National and local campaigns to promote attitude changes, positive role models, and peaceful resolution of conflicts should have age-specific messages. In particular:

- Discouraging violence and aggression, such as corporal punishment at home and in schools.
- Promoting more positive ideas of manhood that value diversity and healthy and stable relationships with the opposite sex.
- Building the skills of young people, their families, and communities to resolve conflicts and reject violence, promoting positive role models and stories.
- Focusing conflict prevention campaigns on violence-prone areas and involving different stakeholders—schools, churches, the media, sports clubs, and parents.

Promoting Youth Inclusion and Participation

Youth inclusion and participation in public policy give young people more choices, enhance their capabilities, and improve their lives and their communities. Integrating youth into the development process as stakeholders and decisionmakers—from consultations to policy, from implementation to evaluation—gives them ownership of the policies and interventions that affect them and enhances national and local development processes. Consideration might be given to:

- Empowering youth to play an active role in the development of their community and the country.

■ Enabling youth to acquire the experience, knowledge, skills, and values necessary for employment and active citizenship.

■ Encouraging youth participation in social accountability initiatives and in the fight against corruption.

■ Providing constructive alternatives to risky behavior and reintegrating marginalized youth.

■ Engaging youth in addressing a wide range of development priorities (combating HIV/AIDS, building sustainable housing, improving literacy rates, mentoring to at-risk youth, building infrastructure, protecting the environment).

Making Public Policies Work for Youth

The long-term youth development strategy should be consistent with national macroeconomic goals, the Millennium Development Goals, and the expected results of poverty reduction strategies and sector investments. To achieve this consistency, policies should:

■ Identify the linkages among interrelated youth outcomes and their common determinants across sectors and age groups.

■ Specify how youth development goals and targets may contribute to national development priorities and embed these goals and targets into i) the national development planning framework; ii) poverty reduction strategies; and iii) relevant sectorwide strategies and programs.

■ Strengthen the links between the long-term youth development vision and the corresponding medium- and short-term strategies, budget allocations, coordination mechanisms, and monitoring and evaluation processes.

Further Policy Directions

In addition, further consideration might be given to the following set of interventions.

Improving Data for More Effective Targeting and Implementation

Effective policies must have measurable risk indicators and reliable data sources to know which youth to target. Building accurate profiles of the challenges youth face is critical for establishing priority outcomes; developing a body of evidence of what works, what does not, and in what circumstances; and advancing policy in a cost-effective way. Consideration should be given to:

Using age-specific, cross-sector data sets and tools to assess the specific risks and opportunities faced by young people. These data sets and monitoring tools should disaggregate youth, addressing their tremendous diversity in age, gender, schooling, marital status, and urban/rural residence. In addition, data should be collected to help identify the most vulnerable, according to the type of youth risk (Types I, II, and III), as well as the key moments to act (such as when a disadvantage is consolidated or when a development opportunity arises).

Improving existing surveys and data systems. Improvements in age-specific data and tools should be embedded into existing systems to avoid creating parallel surveys and data systems. Areas to be explored could be:

- Modifying the Demographic Household Surveys to integrate data for specific youth risk behaviors and their corresponding outcomes (such as questions on domestic violence or crime). The YSCS questionnaire used for this study could serve as an example of how to adapt these surveys.
- Conducting more specialized surveys in disadvantaged areas (such as victimization surveys in low-income urban and rural areas).
- Including recommended youth-focused indicators (in addition to standard education, health, and poverty indicators)—to identify the main issues confronting youth and to serve as an early warning on key problems affecting youth at risk.

Targeting at-risk youth in low-income rural and urban settings more efficiently. Using the improved data, priorities and interventions need to address the specific risks and opportunities of youth:

- Youth affected by HIV/AIDS.
- Indigenous youth.
- Youth in conflict with the law.
- Youth engaged in child labor or working in dangerous circumstances.
- Young female household heads.
- Youth in poor urban and rural areas, with particular attention to the poorest provinces.

Ensuring young people have a voice in designing and implementing policies and interventions that affect them. To set up an effective interface between public sector institutions and youth organizations—encouraging and facilitating their participation and engagement—consideration might be given to:

- *Recognizing youth as stakeholders.* Youth should be recognized as significant stakeholders in public policy, programs, and interventions—from the beginning to the end of the development process. Other key stakeholders—especially those who have an impact on youth and the implementation of youth-focused program interventions—should be involved as well.
- *Expanding the options for youth to engage in political dialogue and national/local development processes.* Establishing spaces and mechanisms for youth participation in national, provincial, and local development planning process (such as the national development plan, provincial and municipal plans, city development strategies, neighborhood/community/slum upgrading programs, and community-driven initiatives).

Enhancing Coordination and Establishing Clear Lines of Accountability across Policies and Sectors that Affect Youth

Identifying youth development synergies and complementarities depends on close cross-sector cooperation and coordination among diverse ministries, institutes, and teams. To ensure that strategic youth concerns and priorities are implemented across government and the country, consideration should be given to the following.

Raising the profile and capability of youth focal points to act as a cross-cutting unit or coordinating mechanism. These should have the mandate, the resources, and the continuity to formulate, coordinate, support, monitor, and evaluate cross-sector youth investments. The focal points should not take over the responsibilities of sector ministries or departments relating to youth but should ensure a youth perspective in the development process. Preparation of youth-focused policies and cross-sector plans depends on the full participation of concerned government agencies and other stakeholders, united around specific goals, targets, and resources for implementing youth investments across the country. The youth focal points should be centers of innovation and expertise on working across sectors on a collaborative basis.

Forging cross-sector collaborations, action plans, and budgets. Sector linkages and cross-cutting issues should be reflected in corresponding action plans, budgets, and implementation arrangements. To achieve this coordination and coherence, consideration might be given to:

- Focusing cross-sector investments and results on comprehensive youth outcomes included in the national planning frameworks.
- Breaking down long-term youth-focused goals and objectives into annual targets and lists of prioritized interventions.
- Specifying youth-focused, cross-sector or sector-specific targets, using measurable indicators.
- Integrating synergies, avoiding overlaps, and ensuring consistency among programs. For instance, second-chance interventions targeting youth at risk should complement programs implemented in the mainstream sectors.
- Allocating timelines and clear lines of responsibility, specifying lead agencies, contributing ministries, and collaborative arrangements.
- Estimating recurrent and capital costs of each intervention, using disaggregated unit costs based on estimates from line ministries, reaching interagency agreements on these unit costs, and avoiding duplication of investments.
- Budgeting and allocating resources to interventions that better reflect cross-sector synergies, have measurable targets, are "implementable" in terms of cross-sector collaborations and agency capacity, and have clear lines of responsibility.

Improving Monitoring and Evaluation

Periodic monitoring and evaluation should be a key component of every youth-focused investment to help policymakers sort out what works and what does not—what is the most cost-effective manner to achieve the objectives, what is harmless but ineffective, and what will actually make the problem worse. Consideration should be given to the following.

Monitoring. An annual "State of Youth" publication that compiles basic indicators for monitoring and communicating progress toward agreed-upon youth outcomes may be a good addition to ongoing monitoring of the implementation of interventions (monitoring the use of inputs and output deliverables of programs).

Evaluation. Because youth outcomes—often the result of cross-sector targeting and collaborations—are more difficult to measure, there is a need to identify both the spillover effects from one youth transition to another and the complementarities across transitions. Quality youth-focused evaluation designs should include:

- Descriptions of the sample's demographic characteristics and risk levels before the intervention.
- Comparison group(s) similar to the treated group(s), using randomization where feasible.
- Good descriptions of the intervention's goals and methods for reducing the risky behaviors.
- A good mix of qualitative and quantitative analysis, including measuring behaviors and effects during and after the intervention.

All these strategies and policies require strong and effective cross-sector, multi-stakeholder collaborations among line ministries, the justice system, municipalities, police, military, courts, prisons, media, community-based organizations, youth organizations, parents, rights-based nongovernmental organizations, schools, universities, sports clubs, private enterprises, churches, and other organizations focused on education, health, and social development.

Argentina at a Glance 2/7/07

Development diamond*

Life expectancy

Gross primary enrollment

GNP per capita

Access to safe water

——— Argentina
------- Upper-middle-income group

POVERTY and SOCIAL	Argentina	Latin America & Carib.	Upper- middle- income
2005			
Population, mid-year (millions)	38.7	551.4	598.7
GNI per capita (Atlas method, US$)	4,470	4,008	5,625
GNI (Atlas method, US$ billions)	173	2,209	3,367
Average annual growth, 1998–2005			
Population (%)	1.0	1.4	0.7
Labor force (%)	2.5	2.4	1.2
Most recent estimate (latest year available, 1995–2006)			
Poverty (% of population below national poverty line)	31	—	—
Urban population (% of total population)	90	77	72
Life expectancy at birth (years)	74	72	69
Infant mortality (per 1,000 live births)	16	27	23
Child malnutrition (% of children under 5)	5	7	7
Access to safe water (% of population)	96	91	94
Illiteracy (% of population age 15+)	97	90	93
Gross primary enrollment (% of school-age population)	112	119	107
Male	113	121	108
Female	112	117	106

(Continued)

Argentina at a Glance 2/7/07 (*Continued*)

KEY ECONOMIC RATIOS and LONG-TERM TRENDS

	1986	1996	2005	2006 (e)
GDP (US$ billions)	110.9	272.1	183.2	210.5
Gross domestic investment/GDP	17.4	18.1	21.5	23.0
Exports of goods and services/GDP	8.2	10.4	24.6	24.6
Gross domestic savings/GDP	19.3	17.4	27.0	28.4
Gross national savings/GDP	—	15.6	24.0	25.7
Current account balance/GDP	–2.6	–2.5	3.2	3.1
Interest payments/GDP	—	2.7	3.6	3.2
Total debt/GDP	47.2	42.0	75	60
Total debt service/exports	82.8	45.6	12.0	30.8
Present value of debt/GDP	—	—	—	—
Present value of debt/exports	—	—	—	—

	1985–95	1995–05	2005	2006 (e)	2006–09 (e)
(avg annual growth)					
GDP	2.2	–1.5	9.2	8.5	5.7
GDP per capita	0.8	0.9	8.2	7.3	4.5
Exports of goods and services	7.5	8.8	16.7	15.2	8.4

Economic ratios*

— Argentina
······· Upper-middle-income group

STRUCTURE of the ECONOMY

(% of GDP)	1986	1996	2005	2006 (e)
Agriculture	7.8	6.0	9.4	8.8
Industry	37.4	28.4	35.6	35.6
Manufacturing	27.4	18.7	23.2	23.2
Services	54.8	65.6	55.0	55.6
Private consumption	..	70.1	61.1	63.1
General government consumption	..	12.5	11.9	8.5
Imports of goods and services	6.3	11.1	19.0	19.2

(average annual growth)	1985–95	1995–05	2005	2006 (e)
Agriculture	2.5	2.7	11.1	8.5
Industry	1.5	2.1	9.2	8.5
Manufacturing	0.9	1.4	7.5	8.5
Services	2.3	1.9	8.4	7.0
Private consumption	..	1.4	7.0	7.2
General government consumption	..	1.4	6.1	8.8
Gross domestic investment	4.1	3.9	22.7	19.2
Imports of goods and services	14.5	5.9	20.1	12.7

Growth of Investment and GDP (%)

GDI — GDP

Growth Rate of Exports and Imports (%)

Exports — Imports

*The diamonds show four key indicators in the country (in bold) compared with its income-group average. If data are missing, the diamond will be incomplete.

Argentina at a Glance 2/7/07 (Continued)

PRICES and GOVERNMENT FINANCE

	1986	1996	2005	2006 (e)
Domestic prices				
(% change)				
Consumer prices	90.1	0.2	12.3	9.8
Implicit GDP deflator	74.5	-0.1	8.8	12.1
Government finance				
(% of GDP, includes current grants)				
Current revenue	21.2	16.9	23.7	24.4
Current budget balance (cash basis)	-1.0	-0.9	3.6	4.0
Overall surplus/deficit (cash basis)	-4.1	-2.1	1.7	1.8

Inflation (%) — GDP deflator, CPI

TRADE

	1986	1996	2005	2006 (e)
(US$ millions)				
Total exports (fob)	6,852	24,043	40,352	46,569
Food	1,245	2,560	2,803	—
Meat	465	1,074	1,642	—
Manufactures	4,778	14,959	25,122	30,052
Total imports (cif)	4,724	23,855	28,689	34,159
Food	—	—	—	—
Fuel and energy	419	922	1,545	1,729
Capital goods	663	5,607	7,011	8,484
Export price index (1993 = 100)	—	116	111	119
Import price index (1993 = 100)	—	106	98	100
Terms of trade (1993 = 100)	—	110	114	120

Exports and Imports (million US$) — Exports, Imports

BALANCE of PAYMENTS

Current Account Balance/GDP (%)

(US$ millions)	1986	1996	2005	2006(e)
Exports of goods and services	8,449	28,448	46,343	53,373
Imports of goods and services	6,906	30,236	34,916	41,838
Resource balance	1,543	−1,787	11,426	11,534
Net income	−4,404	−5,464	−6,207	−5,596
Net current transfers	2	482	570	618
Current account balance	−2,859	−6,769	5,789	6,557
Financing items (net)	1,968	2,887	−14,227	−10,200
Changes in net reserves	891	3,882	8,438	3,643
Memo:				
Reserves including gold (*US$ millions*)	2,905	18,324	27,179	30,000
Conversion rate (*DEC, local/US$*)	9.00E-5	1.0	2.9	3.1

(Continued)

Argentina at a Glance 2/7/07 (Continued)

EXTERNAL DEBT and RESOURCE FLOWS

(US$ millions)	1986	1996	2005	2006 (e)
Total debt outstanding and disbursed	52,450	114,423	135,204	129,209
IBRD	1,140	5,317	6,881	6,206
IDA	0	0	0	0
Total debt service	6,281	12,963	7,420	10,326
IBRD	210	608	1,216	. . .
IDA	0	0	0	0
Composition of net resource flows				
Official grants	—	—	0	0
Official creditors	—	−420	−5,459	−6,720
Private creditors	—	8,117	2,567	2,595
Foreign direct investment	919	4,768	2,983	2,866
Portfolio equity	0	496	−91	−94
World Bank program				
Commitments	499	1,195	495	1,165
Disbursements	408	1,077	362	459
Principal repayments	134	282	928	1,134
Net flows	274	795	−566	−675
Interest payments	75	326	282	340
Net transfers	199	469	−849	−1,015

Composition of 2005 Debt (US$ m.)

A: 6,881
C: 9,768
D: 9,569
E: 2,256
F: 88,714

A - IBRD   B - IDA   C - IMF
D - Other multilateral   E - Bilateral
F - Private   G - Short-term

Source: World Bank, Development Economics department.

References

Assunção, J. 2005. "Brazilian Youth at Risk: Estimating the Costs of Not Preventing Risky Behavior."

Assunçao, J., and L. Carvalho. 2003. "Brazilian Youth at Risk: Estimating the Costs of Not Preventing Risky Behavior." The World Bank, Washington, D.C.

Ayres, I., and S. Levitt. 1998. "Measuring Positive Externalities From Unobservable Victim Precaution: An Empirical Analysis of Lojack." *Quarterly Journal of Economics* 113(1): 43–77.

Barker, G., and M. Fontes. 1996. "Review and Analysis of International Experience with Programs Targeted on Youth At-Risk." LASHC Paper Series 5. The World Bank, Washington, D.C.

Barro, R., and J. Lee. 1993. "International Comparisons of Educational Attainment." *Journal of Monetary Economics* 32(3):363–94.

Beccaria, L., and R. Maurizio. 2003. "Movilidad Ocupacional en Argentina." Colección Investigación. Universidad Nacional de Gral. Sarmiento, Argentina.

———. 2004. "Inestabilidad Laboral en el Gran Buenos Aires." *El Trimestre Económico* 283.

Bermudez, N., and others. 2004. "Representaciones sobre Democracia y Participación en la Juventud de la Ciudad de Cordoba." *Cuadernos FHYCS-UN* 22:129–50.

Binstock, G., and E.A. Pantelides. 2005. "La Fecundidad Adolescente Hoy: Diagnóstico Sociodemográfico." In M. Gogna, ed., *Embarazo y Maternidad en la Adolescencia. Estereotipos, Evidencias y Propuestas para Políticas Públicas.* Buenos Aires: CEDES-Ministerio.

Binstock, G., and M. Cerrutti. 2005. *Carreras Truncadas: El Abandono Escolar en el Nivel Medio en la Argentina.* Buenos Aires: UNICEF.

Bloom, D., and D. Canning. 2005. "Global Demographic Change: Dimensions and Economic Significance." Working Paper 1. Harvard University, Harvard Initiative for Global Health, Cambridge, Mass.

Blum, R. 2006. "Youth at Risk" Workshop. The World Bank, Washington, D.C.

Blum, R.W., L. Halcón, T. Beuhring, E. Pate, S. Campell-Forrester, and A. Venema. 2003. "Adolescent Health in the Caribbean: Risk and Protective Factors." *American Journal of Public Health* 93(3):456–60.

Blum, R., and M. Ireland. 2004. "Reducing Risk, Increasing Protective Factors: Findings from the Caribbean Youth Health Survey." *Journal of Adolescent Health* 35:493–500.

Bozick, R. 2006. "Precocious Behaviors in Early Adolescence." *The Journal of Early Adolescence* 26(1):60–86.

Bronfenbrenner, U. 1979. *The Ecology of Human Development.* Cambridge, Mass.: Harvard University Press.

———. 1986. "Ecology of the Family as a Context for Human Development: Research Perspectives." *Developmental Psychology* 22(6):723–42.

Brooks-Gunn J., G.J. Duncan, P.V.K. Klebanov, and D. Sealand. 1993. "Do Neighborhoods Influence Child and Adolescent Development?" *American Journal of Sociology* 99(2): 353–95.

Buvinic, M., A. Morrison, and M. Shifter. 1999. "Violence in Latin America and the Caribbean: A Framework for Action." Inter-American Development Bank, Washington, D.C.

Cacciamali, M. 2005. "Mercado de Trabajo Juvenil: Argentina, Brasil y México." International Labour Organization.

Calderón, M. 2000. "Job Stability and Labor Mobility in Urban Mexico: A Study Based on Duration Models and Transition Analysis." Latin American Research Network 419. Inter-American Development Bank, Washington, D.C.

Capellari, L., and S. Jenkins. 2002. "Modeling Low Income Transitions." Working Papers 8. Institute for Social and Economic Research, Essex, United Kingdom.

Carlsson, T. 2006. "Youth and Social Development in Argentina—A Survey of the Literature."

CEDLAS. 2004. Website [http://www.depeco.econo.unlp.edu.ar/cedlas/]

CEPAL (Comisión Económica para América Latina y el Caribe). 2004. *La Juventud en Iberoamérica: Tendencias y Urgencias.* Santiago: Comision Economica para America Latina y el Caribe.

Cerimedo, F. 2004. "Duración del Desempleo y Ciclo Económico en la Argentina." Working Paper 8. CEDLAS, Argentina.

Chin-Quee, D., C. Cuthberston, and B. Janowitz. 2006. "Over-the-Counter Pill Provision: Evidence from Jamaica." *Studies in Family Planning* 37(2):99–110.

Coleman, J. 1988. "Social Capital in the Creation of Human Capital." *American Journal of Sociology* 94:95–120.

Contreras, J.M., and R. Hakkert. 2001. "La Sexualidad y la Formación de Unions." In J. Guzmán and others, *Diagnóstico sobre Salud Sexual y Reproductiva de Adolescentes en América Latina y el Caribe.* México: UNFPA.

DEIS (Direccion de Estadisticas e Informacion de Salud). 2005. "Estadisticas Vitales." [http://www.deis.gov.ar/publicaciones/archivos/Serie5Nro49.pdf]

Di Groppelo, E. 2006. *Meeting the Challenges of Secondary Education in Latin America and East Asia: Improving Efficiency and Resource Mobilization.* Washington, D.C.: The World Bank.

Di Marco, G. 2004. "Movimientos Sociales en la Argentina: ¿Reconstrucción de la Sociedad Civil?" Paper Prepared for 2004 meeting of the Latin American Studies Association, Las Vegas, October 7–9.

Dowdney, L. 2005. *Neither War nor Peace: International Comparisons of Children and Youth in Organized Violence.* Rio de Janeiro: COAV.

Fajnzylber, P., D. Lederman, and N. Loayza. 1998. "Determinants of Crime Rates in Latin America and the World: An Empirical Assessment." The World Bank, Washington D.C.

———. 2000. "Crime and Victimization: An Economic Perspective" *Economia* 1(1): 219–78.

———. 2002a. "Inequality and Violent Crime" *Journal of Law and Economics* 65(April): 1–40.

———. 2002b. "What Causes Violent Crime?" *European Economic Review* 46:1323–57.

Fanelli, J. 2003. *The Crisis That Was Not Prevented: Lessons for Argentina, the IMF, and Globalization.* The Hague: FONDAD.

Farber, H. 1999. "Mobility and Stability: The Dynamics of Job Change in Labor Markets." In O. Ashenfelter, ed., *Card Handbook of Labor Economics.* Amsterdam: Elsevier.

FLACSO (Latin American Faculty of Social Sciences). 2006. "Estudio Sobre La Joventud Argentina." Buenos Aires.

Ford Foundation. 2000. "Youth Service. Worldwide Workshop on Youth Involvement as a Strategy for Social, Economic, Democratic Development." Workshop Report. Ford Foundation, New York.

Fundación Banco de la Provincia de Buenos Aires. 2005. "Informe sobre Desarrollo Humano en la Provincia de Buenos Aires 2004–2005." Integración Social de la Juventud.

Galiani, S., and H. Hopenhayn. 2000. "Duración y Riesgo de Desempleo en Argentina." Documento de Trabajo FADE 18. Buenos Aires.

Galiani, S., M. Rossi, and E. Schargrodsky. 2006. "Conscription and Crime." Background paper for *World Development Report 2007*. The World Bank, Washington, D.C.

Garcette, N. 2005. "Property Crime as A Redistributive Tool: The Case of Argentina." Paris School of Economics, Paris.

———. 2006. "Youth, Crime and Violence in Argentina." Background study. The World Bank, Buenos Aires.

Garmezy, N., and M. Rutter. 1983. *Stress, Coping and Development in Children*. Baltimore: Johns Hopkins University Press.

Gayol, S., and G. Kessler. 2002. *Violencias, Delitos Y Justicias En La Argentina*. Buenos Aires: Manatial.

Giovagnoli, P., A. Fiszbein, and H. Partinos. 2004. "Estimating the Returns to Education in Argentina: 1992–2002." Policy Research Working Paper 3715. The World Bank, Washington, D.C.

Giovagnoli, P., I. Kit, M. Marchionni, and J. Paz. 2005. "Urban Female Employment in Argentina." Working Paper 29. CEDLAS-UNLP, Argentina.

Gogna, M. 2005. *Estado del Arte: Investigación sobre Sexualidad y Derechos en la Argentina (1990–2002)*. Buenos Aires: CEDES.

Gogna, M., S. Fernández, and N. Zamberlin. 2005. "Historias Reproductivas, Escolaridad y Contexto del Embarazo: Hallazgos de la Encuesta a Puérparas." In *Embarazo y Maternidad en la Adolescencia. Estereotipos, Evidencias y Propuestas para Políticas Públicas*.

Greenwood, P. 1995. "Juvenile Crime and Juvenile Justice." In J. Wilson and J. Petersilia, eds., *Crime*. San Francisco: Institute for Contemporary Studies.

Guerra, E. 2005. "Citizenship Knows No Age: Children Participation in the Government and Municipal Budget of Barra Mansa, Brazil." *Children, Youth and Environments* 15(2):151–68.

Gupta, R. 2003. "Argentina—What Went Wrong?" *National Accountant*. February/March.

Haggerty, R., L. Sherrod, N. Garmezy, and M. Rutter, eds. 1996. *Stress, Risk and Resilience in Children and Adolescents: Processes, Mechanisms and Interventions*. Cambridge, United Kingdom: Cambridge University Press.

Haile, G. 2004. "Re-employment Hazard of Displaced German Workers." Working Paper 037. Lancaster University Management School, London.

Hanushek, E. 1979. "Conceptual and Empirical Issues in the Estimation of Educational Production Functions." *Journal of Human Resources* 14(3):351–88.

———. 1986. "The Economics of Schooling: Production and Efficiency in Public Schools." *Journal of Economic Literature* 24(3):1141–77.

Haveman, R., and B. Wolfe. 1994. *Succeeding Generations: On the Effects of Investment in Children*. New York: Russell Sage Foundation.

Holzer, H., and R. LaLonde. 1998. "Job Change and Job Stability Among Less-skilled Young Workers." In R. Freeman and H. Holzer, eds., *The Black Youth. Employment Crisis.* Chicago: University of Chicago Press.

Hopenhayn, H. 2001. "Labor Market Policies and Employment Duration: The Effects of Labor Market Reform in Argentina." Latin American Research Network 407. Inter-American Development Bank, Washington, D.C.

IMF (International Monetary Fund). 2003. *Lessons from the Crisis in Argentina.* Washington, D.C.: International Monetary Fund.

———. 2005. "Argentina: 2005 Article IV Consultation." Staff Report, Public Information Notice on the Executive Board Discussion, and Statement by the Executive Director for Argentina. International Monetary Fund, Washington, D.C.

Jimeno, J., and D. Rodriguez-Palenzuela. 2002. "Youth Unemployment in the OECD: Demographic Shifts, Labour Market Institutions, and Macroeconomic Shocks." Working Paper 15. FEDEA, Madrid.

Jones, N., C. Pieper, and L. Robertson. 1992. "The Effect of Legal Drinking Age on Fatal Injuries of Adolescents and Young Adults." *American Journal of Public Health* 82:112–15.

Justesen, M., and D. Verner. 2006. "Haitian Youth." Report 36069–HT. World Bank, Washington, D.C.

———. 2007. "Argentine Youth: Labor Market Response to Economic Fluctuations." World Bank, Washington, D.C.

Kessler, G. 2004. "Sociología del Delito Amateur." Paidos, Buenos Aires.

———. 2005. "Crime, Work and Juvenile Justice in Buenos Aires." Paper presented at the Youth Violence in Latin America conference, London School of Economics, May 27.

Kornblit, A.L., A.M. Mendes Diz, and D. Adaszko. 2006. "Prácticas Sexuales de Jóvenes Escolarizados en Argentina: Relevancia de Su Conocimiento para la Educación Sexual." Paper presented at the conference "V Taller de Investigaciones Sociales en Salud Reproductiva y Sex."

Kuasñosky, S., and D. Szulik. 1996. "Desde los Márgenes de la Juventud." In M. Margulis, ed., *La Juventud es Más que una Palabra: Ensayos sobre Cultura y Juventud.* Buenos Aires: Editorial Biblos.

———. 2000. "Desde los Márgenes de la Juventud." In M. Margulis, ed., *La Juventud es Más Que Una Palabra.* Buenos Aires: Editorial Biblos.

Kugler, A. 2000. "The Incidence of Job Security Regulations on Labor Market Flexibility and Compliance in Colombia: Evidence from the 1990 Reform." Documento de la Red de Centros de Investigación 393. Inter-American Development Bank, Washington, D.C.

Kupets, O. 2005. "Determinants of Unemployment Duration in Ukraine." Working Paper Series 05/01. Economics Research Network, Russia and CIS, Moscow.

LaCava, G., and others. 2004. "Young People in South Eastern Europe: From Risk to Empowerment." Unpublished paper. The World Bank, Washington, D.C.

Lagos, M. 2001. "Between Stability and Crisis in Latin America." *Journal of Democracy* 12(1): 137–45.

Lederman, D. 1999. "Crime in Argentina: A Preliminary Assessment." World Bank, Washington, D.C.

Leighton, L., and J. Mincer. 1982. "Labor Turnover and Youth Unemployment." In R.B. Freeman and D.A. Wise, eds. *The Youth Labor Market Problem: Its Nature, Causes, and Consequences.* Chicago: University of Chicago Press.

Levitt, S., and L. Lochner. 2000. "The Determinants of Juvenile Crime."

Light, A., and M. Ureta. 1992. "Panel Estimates of Male and Female Job Turnover Behavior: Can Female Nonquitters Be Identified?" *Journal of Labor Economics* 10(2): 156–81.

Lule, E., J. Rosen, S. Singh, J. Knowles, and J. Behrman. 2005. "Adolescent Health Programs." In D. Jamison and others, *Disease Control Priorities in Developing Countries.* Bethesda: Disease Control Priorities Project.

Marcus-Delgado, J. 2003. "Trust, Corruption, and the Globalization Tango." *Social Text* 77(21):139–53.

Míguez, H. 2000. "Consumo de Sustancias Psicoactivas en Argentina." *Acta Psiquiátrica y Psicológica de America Latina* 46(3).

———. 2004. "Epidemiología de la Alcoholización Juvenil en Argentina." *Acta Psiquiátrica y Psicológica de América Latina* 50(1):43–47.

Míguez, H., and M.C. Pecci. 1994. "Consumo de Alcohol y Drogas en Jóvenes de Buenos Aires" *Acta Psiquiátrica y Psicológica de América Latina* 40(3):231–35.

Miller, B.C., and K.A. Moore. 1990. "Adolescent Sexual Behaviour, Pregnancy, and Parenting: Research through the 1980s." *Journal of Marriage and the Family* 52(4): 1025–44.

Moller, L. 2002. "Legal Restrictions Resulted in a Reduction of Alcohol Consumption among Young People in Denmark." In R. Room, ed., *Effects of Nordic Alcohol Policy: What Happens to Drinking and Harm When Alcohol Controls Change?* Helsinki: Nordic Council for Alcohol and Drug Research.

Ministerio de Salud. 2005. Boletin sobre el VIH-SIDA en la Argentina. Buenos Aires.

———. 2006. Encuesta Nacional de Factores de Riesgo. Buenos Aires.

Muncie, J. 2005. *Criminology.* London: Sage Publications.

Ohene, S., M. Ireland, and R. Blum. 2005. "The Clustering of Risk Behaviors among Caribbean Youth." *Maternal and Child Health Journal* 9(1):91–100.

O'Malley, P., and A. Wagenaar. 1991. "Effects of Minimum Drinking Age Laws on Alcohol Use, Related Behaviors and Traffic Crash Involvement among American Youth: 1976–1987." *Journal of Studies on Alcohol* 52:478–491.

Pantelides, E.A., and M.S. Cerrutti. 1992. "Conducta Reproductiva y Embarazo en la Adolescencia." *Cuadernos del CENEP* 47.

Pantelides, E.A., R.N. Geldstein, and G. Infesta Domínguez. 1995. "Imágenes de Género y Conducta Reproductiva en la Adolescencia." *Cuadernos del CENEP* 51.

Parsons, D. 1986. "The Employment Relationship: Job Attachment, Work Effort, and the Nature of Contracts." In O. Ashenfelter and R. Layard, eds. *Handbook of Labor Economics.* Amsterdam: North Holland.

Petras, J. 2002. "The Unemployed Workers Movement in Argentina." *Monthly Review* 53(8). [http://www.monthlyreview.org/0102petras.htm]

Plevin, R. 2004. "Vandals in the Name of Love." *A Broad View.* [http://www.abroadview-magazine.com/archives/spring_06/vandals.html]

Ramos, S., and others. 2004. *Para que Cada Muerte Importe.* Buenos Aires: Ministerio de Salud y Ambiente de la Nación-CEDES.

Ravallion, M. 2004. "Evaluating Anti-Poverty Programs." World Bank, Washington, D.C. [http://siteresources.worldbank.org/INTISPMA/Resources/383704-1130267506458/Evaluating_Antipoverty_Programs.pdf.]

Rodgers, D. 1999. "Youth Gangs and Violence in Latin America and the Caribbean: A Literature Survey" LCR Sustainable Development Working Paper 4, Urban Peace Program Series, The World Bank, Washington, D.C.

———. 2005. "Youth Gangs and Perverse Livelihoods Strategies in Nicaragua: Challenging Certain Preconceptions and Shifting The Focus of Analysis" Paper presented at the Arusha conference "New Frontiers of Social Policy," December 12.

Saavedra, J., and M. Torero. 2000. "Labor Market Reforms and Their Impact on Formal Labor Demand and Job Market Turnover: The Case of Peru." Latin American Research Network 394. Inter-American Development Bank, Washington, D.C.

Saraví, G. 2004. "Segregación Urbana y Espacio Público: Los Jóvenes en Enclaves de Pobreza Structural." *Revista de la CEPAL* 83.

Sautu, R., and I. Perugorría. 2004. "Credibility and Trust in Economic and Political Actors and Institutions. Their Effects for the Argentine Democracy." Paper prepared for the 2004 Meeting of the Latin American Studies Association, Las Vegas.

Schudson, M. 1999. *The Good Citizen.* Cambridge, Mass.: Harvard University Press.

Sidicaro, R., and E.T. Fanfani. 1998. *La Argentina de los Jóvenes—Entre la Indifierencia y la Indignación.* Buenos Aires: LOSADA/UNICEF.

Silva, M., and I. Ross. 2003. "Evaluation of a School-based Sex Education Program for Low-income Male High School Students in Chile." *Evaluation and Program Planning* 26(1):1–9.

Sirianni, C. 2005. *The Civic Renewal Movement: Community-building and Democracy in the United States.* Dayton, Ohio: Kettering Foundation Press.

Tedesco, J. 1982. *Educación y Sociedad en la Argentina.* La Plata: CEDLAS.

Torney-Purta, J., R. Lehmann, H. Oswald, and W. Schultz. 2001. "Citizenship and Education in Twenty-Eight Countries: Civic Knowledge and Engagement at Age Fourteen." Amsterdam: International Association for the Evaluation of Educational Achievement.

———. 2003. "Political Democracy and the IEA Study of Civic Education." *Encyclopedia of Education.* 2nd ed. New York: Macmillan.

Udry, J. R. 2003. *The National Longitudinal Study of Adolescent Health (Add Health), Waves I and II, 1994–1996; Wave III, 2001–2002.* Chapel Hill, N.C.: Carolina Population Center, University of North Carolina at Chapel Hill.

Udry, J. R., and B. C. Campbell. 1994. "Getting Started on Sexual Behavior." In S. Rossi and S. Alice, eds., *Sexuality Across the Life Course.* Chicago: University of Chicago Press.

UNAIDS (Joint United Nations Programme on HIV/AIDS). 2006. *Report on the Global AIDS Epidemic.* Geneva.

UNICEF. 2006. *The State of the World's Children.* New York City: UNICEF.

United Nations. 2006. "Report of the Independent Expert for the United Nations Study on Violence against Children." Report A/61/299. United Nations, New York.

UNODC (United Nations Office on Drugs and Crime). 2006. *World Drug Report.*

Verner, D. 2006. "Rural Poor in Rich Rural Areas: Poverty in Rural Argentina." Policy Research Working Paper 4096. The World Bank, Washington, D.C.

Verner, D., and E. Alda. 2004. "Youth at Risk, Social Exclusion, and Intergenerational Poverty Dynamics—A New Survey Instrument with Application in Brazil." Policy Research Working Paper 3296. The World Bank, Washington, D.C.

Weisbrot, M., and A. Cibils. 2002. *Argentina's Crisis: The Cost and Consequences of Default to the International Financial Institutions.* Washington, D.C.: Center for Economic and Policy Research.

WHO (World Health Organization). 2002. *World Report on Violence and Health.* Geneva.

———. 2004a. "World Report on Road Traffic Injury Prevention." WHO.

———. 2004b. *Global Status Report.* Geneva.

Wolfe. 1995. "External Benefits of Education." In M. Carny, ed., *International Encyclopedia of Economics of Education.* Basingstoke: Macmillan.

World Bank. 1999. "Curbing the Epidemic: Governments and the Economics of Tobacco Control." Washington, D.C.

———. 2001. Social Development Notes 62. Washington, D.C.

———. 2003. *Caribbean Youth Development.* Washington, D.C.

———. 2005a. *Argentina: Seeking Sustained Growth and Social Equity.* Washington, D.C.

———. 2005b. *Children and Youth Framework for Action.* Washington, D.C.

———. 2006a. "HIV/AIDS Prevention Among Youth: What Works?" *Children & Youth* 2(1).

———. 2006b. *World Development Report 2007—Development and the Next Generation.* Washington, D.C.

———. 2006c. "Youth-responsive Social Analysis: A Guidance Note. Incorporating Social Dimensions into Bank-supported Projects." Social Analysis Sector Guidance Note Series. Washington, D.C.

———. 2006d. "Youth Service: A Strategy for Youth and National Development." Youth Development Note 2. Washington, D.C.

———. 2008. *Youth at Risk in Latin America and the Caribbean: Understanding the Causes, Realizing the Potential.* Washington, D.C.

World Bank Institute. 2005. "Invertir en Infancia y Juventud: Hacia el Crecimiento Sostenible." Urban and City Management Program (Distance Learning) Course. World Bank, Washington, D.C.

York, J., J. Welte, J. Hirsch, J. Hoffman, and G. Barnes. 2004. "Association of Age at First Drink with Current Alcohol Drinking Variables in a National General Population Sample." *Alcoholism: Clinical and Experimental Research* 28 (9): 1379–87.

Young, M. E., and others. 2000. "From Early Child Development to Human Development." World Bank, Washington, D.C.

Zibechi, R. 2003. *Genealogía de la Revuelta.* Buenos Aires: Nordan-Letra Libre.

Eco-Audit

Environmental Benefits Statement

The World Bank is committed to preserving Endangered Forests and natural resources. We print World Bank Working Papers and Country Studies on 100 percent postconsumer recycled paper, processed chlorine free. The World Bank has formally agreed to follow the recommended standards for paper usage set by Green Press Initiative—a nonprofit program supporting publishers in using fiber that is not sourced from Endangered Forests. For more information, visit www.greenpressinitiative.org.

In 2008, the printing of these books on recycled paper saved the following:

Trees*	Solid Waste	Water	Net Greenhouse Gases	Total Energy
355	16,663	129,550	31,256	247 mil.
'40' in height and 6–8" in diameter	Pounds	Gallons	Pounds CO$_2$ Equivalent	BTUs

IBRD 33362R

BOLIVIA

PARAGUAY

CHILE

BRAZIL

PACIFIC OCEAN

URUGUAY

ATLANTIC OCEAN

ARGENTINA

FALKLAND ISLANDS (ISLAS MALVINAS)
A DISPUTE CONCERNING SOVEREIGNTY OVER THE
ISLANDS EXISTS BETWEEN ARGENTINA WHICH CLAIMS
THIS SOVEREIGNTY AND THE U.K. WHICH ADMINISTERS
THE ISLANDS.

Stanley

TIERRA DEL FUEGO

This map was produced by the Map Design Unit of The World Bank.
The boundaries, colors, denominations and any other information
shown on this map do not imply, on the part of The World Bank
Group, any judgment on the legal status of any territory, or any
endorsement or acceptance of such boundaries.

ARGENTINA

○ SELECTED CITIES AND TOWNS

⊙ PROVINCE CAPITALS

✸ NATIONAL CAPITAL

〜 RIVERS

MAIN ROADS

RAILROADS

PROVINCE BOUNDARIES

— · — INTERNATIONAL BOUNDARIES

AUGUST 2008